PLANTS & GARDENS

BROOKLYN BOTANIC GARDEN RECORD

JAPANESE GARDENS

1990

Brooklyn Botanic Garden

STAFF FOR THE ORIGINAL EDITION:

CLAIRE E. SAWYERS, GUEST EDITOR

BARBARA B. PESCH, EDITOR

STAFF FOR THE REVISED EDITION:

BARBARA B. PESCH, DIRECTOR OF PUBLICATIONS

JANET MARINELLI, ASSOCIATE EDITOR

AND THE EDITORIAL COMMITTEE OF THE BROOKLYN BOTANIC GARDEN

BEKKA LINDSTROM, ART DIRECTOR

JUDITH D. ZUK, PRESIDENT, BROOKLYN BOTANIC GARDEN

ELIZABETH SCHOLTZ, DIRECTOR EMERITUS, BROOKLYN BOTANIC GARDEN

STEPHEN K-M. TIM, VICE PRESIDENT, SCIENCE & PUBLICATIONS

COVER PHOTOGRAPH BY BETSY KISSAM
PHOTOGRAPHS BY ELVIN MCDONALD, EXCEPT WHERE NOTED
BLACK AND WHITE ILLUSTRATIONS COURTESY OF BROOKLYN BOTANIC GARDEN LIBRARY

PLANTS & GARDENS

BROOKLYN BOTANIC GARDEN RECORD

JAPANESE GARDENS

THIS HANDBOOK IS A REVISED EDITION OF PLANTS & GARDENS, VOL. 41, No. 3

HANDBOOK # 108

The steps of Mitsui Garden are bordered by clipped boxwood and blooming azaleas.   PHOTO BY GEORGE TALOUMIS

LETTER FROM THE BOTANIC GARDEN

BARBARA B. PESCH

apanese views on gardening have been of major interest here at the Brooklyn Botanic Garden, and evidently to the readers of *Plants & Gardens* as well, for our handbooks on bonsai continue to head our list of best sellers. The previous handbook entitled "Japanese Gardens and Miniature Landscapes," completed in 1961, went through numerous printings before the present entirely new edition was completed.

In the pages that follow you will find many references to tranquility, peace, and quiet beauty. Perhaps it is the search for these qualities in our pressure ridden, fast-paced lives that generates the interest in Japanese gardens here in the States.

BBG's own Japanese Hill-and-Pond Garden was designed and constructed by Takeo Shiota in 1914-15 and remains today a focal point. Throughout the entire year this garden provides a panorama of peace and beauty. Flowers are used with restraint and the evergreen trees and shrubs, in association with rocks and water, present an ever-changing vista as paths are traveled. To the Japanese each garden is designed to mirror nature—it is a landscape in condensed form.

Claire Sawyers, who has lived and worked in Japan, has gathered together a particularly talented group of contributors for this issue. All bring expertise from their fields of concentration to enlighten the reader on every aspect of understanding the art of the Japanese garden. The contributors have related their personal experiences, personal viewpoints and opinions, and first-hand knowledge to provide new insights into this garden phenomenon. Sometimes it is easier to see through someone else's eyes than to see with our own eyes, and these authors indeed have keen vision.

Whether you wish to create a Japanese garden or just gain better understanding of their meaning, we wish you good reading and good gardening. 🌱

Above: Robert Gundacker, gardener in charge of BBG's Japanese Garden.

ROCKS, ISLANDS, MOUNTAINS, AND THE JAPANESE GARDEN

T. Kaori Kitao

A Japanese Garden may be created without flowers, grass, ponds, streams, mounds, paths, and even trees and shrubs, but a Japanese garden cannot exist without rocks. They appear in every conceivable size and shape and arrangement. There are boulders and fist-size stones, smooth or rough. Some are covered with moss, others are tall and soaring, while still others are flat and sprawling. They appear in rows or in clusters, strung out to form a water's edge and sometimes strewn in profusion to simulate a rocky landscape; or half buried in grass, they may escape our glance; or a single lonely stone, seemingly abandoned, may intrude into a path to draw attention. Rocks can be composed as a stone lantern, and carved to form water basins.

In Japan, rocks are not just rocks; they are privileged objects, objects that demand very special attention. When the

Japanese discuss rocks, they discuss them with reverence, considering each rock individually, identifying features and exercising the critical discrimination of a collector of works of art. Shape, aspect, colors, and grains of each rock, and even its force and energy and the sense of presence are considered. Starting with the 11th-century manual, *Sakuteiki*, the art of choosing, laying and arranging rocks has been closely studied.

Rocks, Islands, Mountains

The fascination the Japanese hold for rocks is a deep-rooted cultural phenomenon, and its sources can be located in Japan's topography, mythology, and early literary iconography.

Japan is a volcanic archipelago, two-thirds of which consists of mountains. Its coastline is jagged, rocky, and strewn with innumerable islands. Mountains, islands, and rocks form a continuum as visual forms. Islands are, after all, rocky mountains in water.

Rocky coasts, on the other hand, are not unique to Japan. But the spiritual outlook of the Japanese toward the rocks

T. Kaori Kitao, *Professor of Art History, Swarthmore College, Swarthmore, PA, teaches a range of subjects. She is currently researching the Japanese garden as an index of Japanese culture.*

that surround them is something special, and Japanese mythology is informative on this point.

Rocks as Sacred Dwellings

Some of the oldest archeological remains in Japan, from the Middle Jomon Period (ca. 2000 BC) are arrangements of radially placed natural stones with an upright stone at their centers — unmistakably phallic in form and meaning. The belief was most probably that the god of procreation dwelt in the stone. In the Shinto worship, with its strong strain of animism, gods or spirits dwell in everything everywhere. In its most primitive form, however, the indigenous Japanese religion entertained the notion of mononoke — literally, "the spirit of things." Rocks were seen as the dwelling places of the deities. To this day there are certain rocks, individually or in a group, in the precincts of some older shrines, which are so designated with hallowed ropes and paper; they are called iwakura ("rock-seat"); or, if the whole area around is marked, iwasaka ("rock zone").

To the Japanese, then, rocks are ubiquitous, and yet they also invoke a sense of reverence and even religious awe as though they hold the mystery of life and nature. The ancient Japanese believed, in fact, that rocks grew. This idea is repeated in the poem which is sung today as the Japanese anthem: "may the nation live and thrive thousands of years till the pebbles have grown to be boulders covered with moss." To the Japanese rocks have always been simple and humble and yet divine, and at the same time awesome and familiar.

Literary Sources

Skeptics may still argue, however, that it is not uncommon in primitive religions that trees, rocks and mountains are imbued with mystery and viewed with awe.

The unification of Japan by the Yam-ato clan took place in the 5th century, and thence comes the earliest evidence of Japanese literature. The poets of the day praised the three mountains of the Yamato basin, Kagu and Miminashi, both male, flanking the female Unebi, none very tall but often seen floating above the mist which collects in the area. The Inland Sea with its numerous islands and rocky shores was equally important in the cultural life of early Japan because it was a chief channel of communication. Its image was surely well etched in the memories of many travelers and poets.

Garden as Island

The mountain is sacred in many other cultures as well. But in Japan, topography and mythology worked in consort to reinforce the literary iconography, and it is the merging of the mountain with the rock and the island that is unique and of special significance to the history of the Japanese garden.

In the writings of the 7th and 8th centuries (Nara Period), the garden was called *shima* which is the same word as "island." We know, too, that the earliest Japanese garden featured a mound and a pond and an islet connected to the shore by a bridge; Emperor Shomu (724-29) is said to have had three such gardens in Nara. Thenceforth, the garden, called *shima* or not, could not be conceived without rocks and mounds signifying not only islands but also mountains.

The Mountain of Immortals

To complicate the matter further, however, the influx of Chinese culture in Japan during the Nara Period gave the iconography of the island overlays of Taoist and Buddhist sources which concerned mountains. They are the *horaisan* and the *shumisen*.

Horaisan, or Mt. Horai, as understood in Japan, is a Taoist island-mountain of eternal youth, a sort of Elysium or Par-

Brooklyn Botanic Garden's own Hill-and-Pond Garden illustrates one of the oldest Japanese garden styles. Hills and a pond were created to suggest mountains and ocean.

adise. The legend goes that in 221 B.C. the first emperor of China, Ch'in Shih Huang-ti, dispatched Hsu Fu to Mt. Horai in pursuit of the elixir of life to be found on this island of immortals. But, as it happened, he landed in Japan and never returned home. He settled there with the youths and maidens who accom-panied him and eventually died there.

Horaisan is, for the Japanese, the leg-endary Japan and yet a mythical place as well, believed to be inhabited by cranes and tortoises, both creatures of excep-tional longevity, and covered with pines, peaches and plums, also known to live and grow for many centuries. These are all familiar themes that continue to recur in Japanese gardens as well as in literature, theater, and various festive and religious iconography.

Shumisen, or Mt. Sumeru, is the center of the world in Buddhist cosmology. It is a sacred mountain somewhat analogous to Olympus, the summit of which is the dwelling of Taishakuten, one of the 12 guardian deities. As early as 657 AD, according to the ancient chronicle *Nihongi*, a model of the mountain was constructed at the Asuka Temple near Nara. It was this stone "statue," known as yamagata ("mountain-form"), which shumisen referred to in particular in Japan, especially in garden design. The stone was actually excavated in 1902.

The *shumisen* and the *horaisan* have thus enriched the image of the rock as an island-mountain; and through the history of the Japanese garden, they remained fused in the general iconography of the rock.

Bamboo spout carries water to a basin shaped like an old Oriental coin.

Multiple Meaning

It always baffles Japanese to be asked what the rocks in Japan's gardens mean. For, on the one hand, there is no simple answer to the question; and, on the other, it seems so self-evident as to require no explanation. Used in the garden, a rock may be a *shumisen*, a *horaisan*, a particular island scene, or simply any mountain; or it may be just a rock, nothing more and nothing less. But whatever the specific reference, it cannot be understood free of the multiple images from the topographical, mythological, and literary history that constitute its iconography: the rock as island, as mountain, as holy place, as garden. Whatever its specific reference, the rock is something that immediately and inescapably appeals to the Japanese. And, for the most part, a Japanese does not have to be well read in classics or versed in mythology and archeology to sense that, for it is

an iconography that survives — in the inevitable cultural circularity — in Japan's gardens, which serve as literature and mythology in living form. In this way, rocks form an integral part of Japan's collective memory — their multiple meanings implicit. 🍎

A stone with a hollow serves as a water basin.

BASIC JAPANESE GARDEN STYLES

STEPHEN A. MORRELL

When viewing a Japanese garden, first consider that several distinct styles exist. As with most garden styles, however, the influence of one style can be seen on another. In the West this is often planned; different styles of Japanese gardens are blended together in attempts to capture everything.

The Japanese describe many garden styles, but there are five basic styles. First is one of the oldest styles, the "Hill and Pond Garden," which constitutes the main body of Japanese garden styles of which there are many variations. Here nature is represented by artificially constructed hills and pond, suggesting mountains and ocean. Shrubs are trimmed to complement the undulating contours of mountains and clouds, as well as to maintain scale. Trees are kept pruned and trained to look old and windswept and a major portion of the garden can be seen from any one point. It is understandable why this style is

STEPHEN A. MORRELL, *Curator of the John P. Humes Japanese Stroll Garden on Long Island, is a graduate of the New York Botanical Garden School of Horticulture. He went on a study tour of Japan, seeing gardens as well as collecting plants.*

prominent since it resembles the natural landscape of Japan.

Second, the *karesansui* or "Dry Landscape" garden, traditionally associated with Zen temples, is usually a small space created as an aid to meditation where nature is reduced and suggested using only stones, raked gravel,* and a minimum of plants. The technique of *shakkei* or "borrowed scenery" is often used by incorporating a distant vista as a background of the design, thereby perceptually enlarging the size of the garden. (The borrowed scenery technique is also used in other garden styles.) In Japan, dry gardens are viewed from a veranda and not entered as this would ruin the delicate relationship and scale of the composition. Variations of this style are often found incorporated into other styles in the West.

Third, the tea garden or *Roji*, literally meaning "Dewy Path," is simply a stepping stone path modeled after a mountain trail leading to, and providing a setting for, the teahouse. The path features a stone lantern which is lit for evening tea gatherings and a stone water basin where guests rinse their mouths and hands in an act of purifying body

"SHIN" (ELABORATE) STYLE OF HILL GARDEN, FROM AN ILLUSTRATION IN "TSUKIYAMA TEIZŌ-DEN"

and mind before entering the teahouse. The use of stepping stones, stone lanterns, and water basins in gardens originated with the teagarden and these are common components in later garden styles. Plants in a teagarden are mostly evergreens creating a subdued atmosphere conducive to appreciating the tea ceremony. The teagarden and Dry Landscape garden, or variations of them, have become increasingly popular because their small size and simplicity make them practical.

The fourth style, the "Stroll" garden, takes advantage of tea garden techniques by incorporating stepping stones, stone lanterns, and usually a tea house or pavilion. Traditionally they were created by the nobility and designed on a large scale. Movement is around a pond and islands, employing the concepts of "Hide and Reveal" and "Movement Along the Diagonal." Rather than follow a straight axis, the path leads one left and right to reveal vistas gradually as one moves through the garden. Contrasting with the other garden styles, the entire Stroll garden cannot be viewed from any one point and requires active participation to experience it fully.

The fifth style, which is now very popular in Japan due to space limitations, is the "Courtyard" garden. Here, the strong influence of the tea garden and Dry Landscape garden can be seen. This style is not yet common in the West.

A Japanese garden strives to be true to the essence of nature, a beauty that is quiet and refined. It has a static quality which is maintained by the predominance of stone and evergreen plants, and yet is constantly changing. Through the passing of seasons, change is expressed, and over time quality and depths are reflected by the effects of weathering. The spirit of a Japanese garden is not easy to comprehend fully by viewing its physical elements only. The design encourages one to look deeper and complete the picture in one's own mind. 🍃

*Frequently the word "sand" is used in reference to *karesansui* gardens, but the gravel is more like a turkey grit.

11

A leaf strewn path in autumn at the Brooklyn Botanic Garden's
own Hill-and-Pond Garden.

CLASSICAL PLANTS IN JAPANESE HORTICULTURE

BARRY YINGER

Since the opening of Japan to the West in the last century, countless books and articles have been published about the aesthetics and practice of Japanese horticulture. Most describe and illustrate the Japanese gardens, especially those of the nobility or the great shrines and temples. Some of these works successfully illustrate and interpret the development of the gardens of the privileged, but they scarcely touch the heart of Japanese horticulture: plants. The Japanese people grow a staggering variety of ornamental plants, perhaps more than any other nation, and have at the same time conceived some of the world's most beautiful and emotionally evocative gardens by using a very limited variety of plants. Some very fine gardens use no plants at all. What do they do with all those plants? The answers to that question lead to the heart of Japanese horticulture.

The famous gardens of Japan have not been an immediate part of the ordinary Japanese citizen's horticultural experience. Until recently most important gardens were open only to the elite,

BARRY YINGER, *a graduate of the University of Maryland, College Park, was Curator of Asian Collections at the U.S. National Arboretum in Washington, D.C. He also holds an M.S. in Ornamental Horticulture from the University of Delaware's Longwood Program. He has conducted ten plant explorations in Japan, one in Taiwan, and four in South Korea.*

and even now access to many is greatly restricted. In any case, very few Japanese families, past or present, have more than a tiny scrap of garden space; many have none at all. Instead they have used the odd spaces at curbside and balconies and fire escapes. There is no limit to the Japanese ability to maintain an exciting array of plants in cramped and difficult surroundings. I have seen tubs of Japanese iris (*Iris ensata* var. *ensata*) on grimy curbs in industrial neighborhoods, blooming pots of the orchid *Cypripedium macranthum*, and the shrub *Menziesia ciliicalyx* var. *purpurea* at the base of vending machines on a busy street; more than 50 selections of Japanese maple (*Acer palmatum* and *A. japonicum*) in rows of pots on the roof of a store; and nearly 100 different selections of the epiphytic orchid *Dendrobium moniliforme* in tiny pots in layered wire racks on the small balcony of an apartment house.

Koten engei Defined

Much of this pot culture of ornamental plants is simply horticultural exuberance, but some falls into the category of *koten engei*. The term *koten engei* is difficult to translate precisely, but "cultivation of classical plants" comes close. It is the cultivation of selections of a limited number of plant species in pots according to certain rules and conventions.

Koten engei is one of many branches of

13

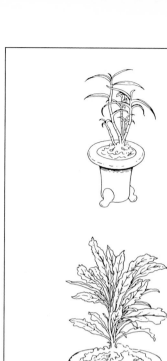

Above left: *Dendrobium moniliforme*
Above right: *Rohdea japonica*
Middle: *Ardisia japonica*
Below left: *Rhapis excelsa*
Below right: *Psilotum nudum*

DRAWINGS BY DONALD EMMINGER.
USED BY PERMISSION OF THE AUTHOR.

Japanese aesthetics in which a foreign model has been accepted, elaborated and gradually transformed into something distinctly Japanese. In this case, as in many others, the model was Chinese. Throughout Chinese history, selections of plants with showy flowers were grown in decorative pots to be used as temporary displays indoors and out. These plants, such as the peony (*Paeonia suffruticosa*) and chrysanthemum, were selected for color and form of their flowers. This concept was imported by the Japanese in the Heian Period (794-1192 AD) when Chinese influence shaped the aesthetics of Heian court society. Chinese-style pot culture was gradually transformed into the practice of growing myriad selections of certain species of native Japanese plants with subtle variations in leaf shape and pattern. The history of this transformation offers important insights into Japanese attitudes about ornamental plants.

The History of *Koten engei*

In the early years of the Heian Period the Japanese approach to aesthetics could be summarized by the concept of *miyabi*, best defined as "refinement and sophistication" from the point of view of a Japanese court society eager to isolate itself from the ignorant masses. The sumptuous elegance of court society in the Chinese style was a refuge not only from the common people, but also from the simple, rustic style of life that was later glorified by Japanese poets and artists. But the peace and stability of Heian times deteriorated into warfare and chaos as Japan endured nearly uninterrupted civil war from 1100 to 1800 AD.

One reaction to the horror of war and social disorder was a new approach to aesthetics, sometimes summarized by the term *yugen* which marked a retreat from glitter and ostentation. *Yugen* empha-sized the profound and mysterious, along with the value of simple forms stripped of distracting ornamentation. The term *sabi* also appeared, describing the pleasure which can be found in weathered or faded things.

This different approach came to be expressed in garden art and horticulture, and set the stage for the appreciation of the kinds of modest plants that came to be embraced by *koten engei*. The critical development that spurred this changed attitude toward beauty in plants was the development of the tea ceremony and its structure and gardens.

The tea ceremony developed as a peaceful refuge for men overwhelmed by the violence of their lives and times, leading them to a keen appreciation of a simple, rustic retreat within turbulent cities. The tea garden developed as a device to establish a mood of contemplation in the guests who passed through it to the tea house. Showy flowers were banished, replaced by humble herbs and shrubs which had previously been grown for medicinal and religious reasons near the dwellings of commoners and in the precincts of *Shinto* shrines. The sophisticated urban dweller now rejected the glittering complexity of the Heian court in favor of rustic materials and a simple style of floral decoration. Most of the species of plants which came to be part of *koten engei* were grown, or were suitable (in their original form) to be grown in the tea garden.

In 1603, Japan was united under the first Tokugawa *shogun*, Ieyasu, who ruled from the new capital at Edo (Tokyo). He and subsequent Tokugawa *shoguns* stimulated the development of the cult of *koten engei*. Ieyasu himself was an avid collector of plants at his home at Suruga. One of those plants was *Asarum* (wild ginger), which was also depicted in the family crest of the Tokugawa family.

Ieyasu's successor, Hidetada, also an

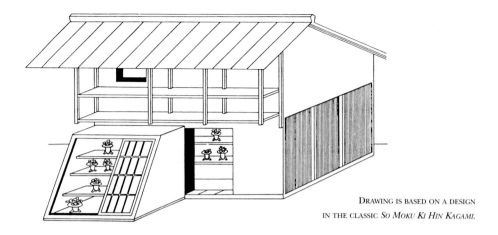

DRAWING IS BASED ON A DESIGN
IN THE CLASSIC *SO MOKU KI HIN KAGAMI*.

A structure for the display and winter storage of *koten engei* plants. The wide roof on the display section protects the plants from the afternoon sun.

avid plant collector, ordered officials throughout Japan to bring him unusual plants. The custom of presenting plant mutations to the *shogun* quickly spread throughout the ranks of *samurai* and powerful citizens. We can be sure that *Asarum* and other *koten engei* subjects were among the plants presented.

The third *shogun*, Iemitsu (1623 to 1651) was an even more avid plantsman than his predecessors. A book of 100 camellia cultivars, *Hyakuchinshu*, was published during his rule. Most important was his establishment of the system of alternate residence, under which all the landed nobility throughout Japan were required to spend part of each year in residence in Edo (Tokyo). Iemitsu encouraged these vassal *daimyo* to bring interesting plant mutations to Edo and assemble to discuss them.

The system of alternate residence stimulated the rise of a class of educated, moneyed commoners on the fringes of this uprecedented concentration of idle *daimyo* and their many retainers. The development of the "floating world" (*ukiyo*) to provide for their entertainment and comfort stimulated the democratization of art and entertainment. *Kabuki* theater, *haiku* poetry and woodblock printing (*ukiyo-e*) owe the strength of their popularity to the vigor and interest of the rising middle class.

Two related developments in ornamental horticulture are characteristic of this period in Japanese history: the evolution of the courtyard garden (*tsuboni-wa*) and the rise of the mania for collecting mutations and variations of ornamental plants. Urban commoners, lacking the spacious estates of the nobility, distilled the tea garden into the *tsuboni-wa* to make use of small enclosed spaces among their houses. They retained the most emotional symbols of the tea garden: the stone lantern to light the way, the stepping stones to provide an unsoiled path, and the water basin to clean hands and mouth. This simple garden might be almost bare of plants, or include at most a few subdued trees, shrubs or herbs.

This movement to sparse, emotionally-charged gardens directly contradicted the simultaneous development of interest in the often bizarre mutations of a wide variety of plants. Because such plants had no place in the garden, and because collectors wished to grow many different kinds of plants in a very limited space, their mutations were normally grown and displayed in small pots. Weak or slow-growing selections were more suitable for long-term pot culture than vigorous relatives.

The Conventions of *Koten engei*

It is hard to say when unrestrained collecting of plant mutations came to be so ruled by convention that *koten engei* could be recognized as a distinct horticultural movement. We, like the Japanese who tried to define the movement in the last century, can only consider it in hindsight. Those who collected mutations in the past three centuries probably did not realize the rules they composed for selection and cultivation of mutations would become the conventions of a persistent horticultural movement. As there is no chronicle of the ideas and emotions of those who developed *koten engei*, we must look to the characteristics of the *koten engei* plant groups that have persisted to the present to understand it.

The following species are the original forms which have spawned the groups of selections most commonly grown as *koten engei* today:

Ardisia japonica (yabukoji)
Ardisia crenata (manryo)
Asarum spp. *(saishin)*
Cymbidium goeringii (shunran)
Dendrobium moniliforme (chosei ran)
Nandina domestica (nanten)
Neofinetia falcata (fuki ran)
Psilotum nudum (matsubaran)
Rhapis excelsa (kannon chiku)
Rohdea japonica (omoto)
Selaginella tamariscina (iwa hiba)

These species share several features:

1. All are Japanese natives which in their original forms are not showy.

2. The cultivated variants of the species are selections (aberrant forms) rather than hybrids. Except in some selections of *Cymbidium* and *Neofinetia* (orchids), selection is for characteristics other than flower form and color, and even those selected for floral characteristics are not very showy. Most selections are for variation in leaf form and color, especially variegated patterns. Many of the variations would be considered inconsequential by Western standards.

3. The selection of variants is not haphazard. Different kinds and degrees of variation have been classified and given names, and some are judged more desirable than others. Usually those aberrations which weaken a plant's constitution and increase its dependence on its grower's skill are most desirable.

4. The selections are always grown and displayed in pots, not in the garden. The traditional pot is of *raku* ware, a thin porous container fired at low temperature, with a rough surface and a shiny black glaze. The pots are decorated with a gold rim and feet (*fuchikin*), waves and birds (*nami-nishiki*), or elaborate patterns of flowers or fantastic animals (*nishiki*).

5. The selections are assigned names which are usually metaphorical, or sometimes allusions to places or events in classical Chinese history. These names are usually written in Chinese characters rather than the Japanese phonetic systems (*kana*).

6. The cultivars are evaluated by societies of hobbyists who deal with the selections of one species. The results of evaluation are periodically published on a chart called a *meikan* which resembles the traditional scoreboard (*banzuke*) of *sumo* wrestling.

7. Interest in the various groups is cyclical and has been accompanied by waves of intense financial speculation as prices rise in times of popularity.

The Cultivation of *Asarum*

The development of *koten engei* as a horti-

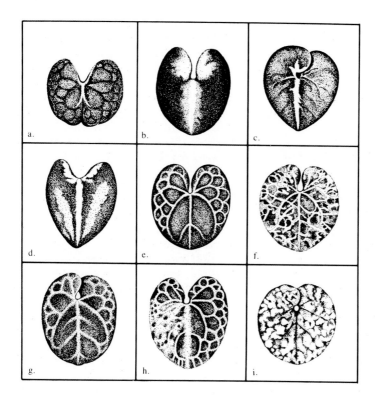

Some leaf characteristics (*gei*) used in classification of *Asarum* selections.

a. *biri o otsu:* leaf tip strongly relfexed; *uchidashi:* deeply sunken veins

b. *tamafu:* large central variegated area (jewel variegation)

c. *tani* and *cho:* central stripe and markings at base (valley and butterfly)

d. *sagari fuji:* diagonal stripes of variegation on both sides of the leaf (hanging wisteria)

e. *kikko:* large network of variegation following veins (tortoise shell)

f. *nagarefu:* irregular indistinct variegation

g. *eriawase:* overlapping basal lobes

h. *zu:* asymmetrical yellow or white irregular variegation (map)

i. *gomafu:* small regular spots of variegation (sesame variegation)

cultural movement can be better comprehended by looking closely at one of the groups cultivated such as *Asarum* (wild ginger). Japanese awareness of *Asarum* dates to the beginning of Japanese history, as seen by the carved *Asarum* designs at the eaves of ancient buildings. These designs were thought to protect buildings from thunderstorms and earthquakes. The species of *Asarum* which is of most interest in the development of the selections, *Asarum takaoi*, grows in profusion at the approach to the grand shrine at Ise, the most revered of ancient *Shinto* shrines. *Asarum* can be seen growing in a variety of gardens in Kyoto where quiet, rustic, understated elegance characterizes the plantings. Its religious and ornamental importance is entwined with its medicinal properties,

and it is still important in Chinese-style pharmacology. *Shinto* priests, like their Korean *shaman* predecessors, decorated their costumes and headdresses with *Asarum* leaves.

Koten engei in the U.S.

What does *koten engei* have to do with the All-American Gardener? Probably more than you realize. The Japanese garden as a setting for mental repose, and the involvement in close-up cultivation of highly dependent plants have taken root in Japan largely because of their role in "stress management" in crowded urban societies. Quiet retreats and "high-touch" horticulture are as relevant to American urbanites today as they were to ravaged *samurai* in Nagoya. 🌿

18

THE TIE BETWEEN JAPANESE ARCHITECTURE AND GARDENS

Harriet A. Henderson

Japanese architecture and gardens are characterized by highly integrated indoor and outdoor spaces. This integration can be traced through the history of Japanese buildings and gardens.

Historical Development

Shinto and Buddhist religions greatly influenced the form of Japanese gardens and architecture. To summon the Shinto *kami*, gods believed to dwell in mountains, rivers and throughout the natural environment, a holy space was prepared. Consisting of four wood columns marking a square on a plane of white sand, this sacred space influenced the development of Japanese dwellings and the dry landscape gardens known as *karesansui.*

The arrival of Buddhism in the 7th century brought Chinese architecture and city planning, with vermilion red buildings grouped symmetrically along north-south axes. Gradually, the Japanese assimilated and transformed these symmetrical arrangements to accommodate the natural mountainous topography. Buildings were placed on diagonal axes, with the staggered structures creating spaces for gardens around each pavilion. As the vibrant Chinese colors were replaced with the natural Japanese wood surface on the structures, the formal Chinese courtyards gave way to more informal and asymmetrical Japanese gardens. Gardens in the 8th to 12th centuries typically represented a Buddhist paradise with a pond and flowering plants, and they were also enjoyed for boating and poetry readings.

During the 13th and 14th centuries, architectural innovations included *shoji* sliding doors (opaque paper panels within wood lattice frames) and *fusuma* (paper covered sliding panels, which were often painted). Rounded columns replaced the four square columns which established the corners of a room. Eventually, *tatami* (woven floor mats about 3 feet by 6 feet) were used as floor coverings, and the dimensions of the assembled *tatami* determined the overall shape of the room.

HARRIET A. HENDERSON, *a landscape architect, is currently employed with Johnson, Johnson and Roy, Inc. in Dallas, Texas. She studied at Kyoto University and traveled in Japan on a Cornell Fellowship.*

19

This Memphis house and garden are tied together by the use of natural materials — bricks and wood. The collection of bonsai fits nicely along the rails of the porch.

In the 15th and 16th centuries, Zen Buddhism reached the peak of its influence. With its emphasis on simplicity, Japanese architecture and gardens became increasingly subdued. In temples, rock and sand gardens with evergreen plants were preferred for contemplation and meditation. Designed to be viewed from the building in a kneeling or sitting position, some gardens expressed the stark beauty of Chinese landscape paintings, while others reflected the Zen asceticism through abstract compositions.

Following the Zen philosophy, founders of the tea ceremony modeled the tearoom after the rustic thatched roof farmhouse to create an atmosphere of seclusion from the rigid patterns of daily life. The path to the tearoom was designed to evoke the feeling of a journey to a mountain retreat. Out of this tradition, with its emphasis on the path-

way and movement, developed the stroll garden in which pavilions, usually located around a pond, were linked by paths.

Throughout Japanese history, the design of the architecture and gardens has been influenced by the climate and the abundance of natural resources. To ease the humidity of the summers and the threat of earthquakes, the houses are elevated 1-1/2 to 2-1/2 feet above the ground on wood columns, with flexible partitions. The sliding screens are adjusted to create large or small open spaces according to the season and to frame views of the garden. Large overhanging roofs of clay tile, wood shingles or thatch provide relief from the sun and rain.

The enclosure of the house and garden by a wall or fence, the area under the eaves and the sliding partitions of

The viewing pavilion in the Brooklyn Botanic Garden's
Japanese Garden represents the home of the host and affords
the best views of the garden.

buildings are three important features which illustrate how traditional Japanese buildings and gardens are integrated.

To create a private domestic space separated from the densely populated outside world, each lot is surrounded by an enclosing wall, fence or hedge that is above eye level. The house and garden are linked by the surrounding enclosure. The materials used reflect the natural resources readily available and set a tone of formality or informality. Stone walls and tile-topped clay walls tend to be formal and architectural, while wood, bamboo and reed fences vary from geometric to asymmetrical patterns. Hedges are often used in combination with open weave bamboo fences as a subtle transition from the garden to the enclosing edge. Berms also screen unwanted views while providing a change of topography within the garden.

The Japanese also enclose the garden to frame desired views with walls, fences, and plants. Focusing on a neighboring tree, nearby hill, or landscape feature gives the illusion of a larger garden by "borrowing scenery," or *shakkei*.

Another example of enclosure which links the building to the garden is the sleeve fence — a direct extension of the building. Made of bamboo and dried reeds, this fence has dimensions which are generally five to six feet high and three feet wide. The sleeve fence leads the viewer's eye from the building out into the garden, and it makes a transition in materials from the planned wood of the structure to the plants in the garden.

In the area under the eaves, the second important feature, the line of the roof overhang is repeated on the ground in stone, as a 12 to 18 inch wide gravel band edged with cut stone or rock. This run-off area for drainage is as decorative a part of the garden as it is a functional part of the house. Ornamental bronze or iron rain-chains hung from the overhang corners act as vertical accents and allow rain water, dancing down the chains, to become a decorative garden element. As these gravel and stone bands follow the rectilinear building lines, a contrasting stepping stone path with an irregular pattern leads from the garden to the edge of the house. The stepping stone at the building entrance is used for placing shoes before entering the house, and it is larger and higher than the other stepping stones.

Traditionally, the wood columns of the house and the posts supporting the overhang rest on stone bases to protect the wood from moisture. A natural rock or cut stone column base is often used today as a decorative transition from the architecture to the garden.

A raised wood veranda, typically under the overhang, can be used as an extension of the living area, or as part of the garden since it generally has no handrails. The bamboo and wood used for the veranda contrast in texture to the *tatami* and *shoji* of the interior, while harmonizing with the exterior rocks, plants, fences, and stone walls.

When the space under the eaves is kept at ground level, it assumes even more of the character of the garden. A change of surface to cut stone or gravel often occurs in this intermediate area to indicate the transition from the exterior to the interior. In some cases there is a complete integration of house and garden with plants brought into the vestibule area as part of a flush planter or in containers. There, the steps inside signal the beginning of the interior spaces and the location to place shoes.

Screening devices, such as rattan blinds known as *sudare,* are often hung from the eaves to shield the veranda from sunlight or unpleasant views. They provide ways for the inhabitants to see or experience nature, while still protecting them from the elements.

In both the veranda and vestibule areas, moveable wooden shutters, glass panels, and *shoji* screens further blend the interior and exterior spaces. All of these sliding partitions extend from floor to ceiling, and when opened provide uninterrupted expanses for viewing the garden. The outer heavy wood shutters provide protection, privacy, and insulation at night, but they can be opened and stored in the wall during the day. Glass doors with wood frames provide views of the garden, while shielding the interior during inclement weather. The *shoji* can be drawn back to open an entire room to a garden panorama, with the interior wood hewn columns echoing the tree trunks in the garden. With equal ease, *shoji* can also be partially closed to frame a specific garden feature. When completely closed, the *shoji* transmit soft, filtered light, and the pattern of branch and leaf shadows cast on the sliding doors still reveals the presence of the exterior landscape.

The integrated design of Japanese architecture and gardens offers many interesting ideas on how to fuse houses and gardens. The transition from the house to the garden is made by moving from refined materials with architectural designs, to rough hewn and natural materials with asymmetrical patterns. Innovative ways of enclosing indoor and outdoor spaces are shown with an array of fences, walls, and partitions. An intermediate space of a veranda or vestibule extends the garden into the house, and the house into the garden. The flexible partitions not only delineate the space and views from room to room and from room to garden, but also allow an openness and unity between the interior and exterior. ❧

JAPANESE GARDENS

THE VIEW FROM THE WILDERNESS

JOHN L. CREECH

There is a special aspect of Japanese gardens that commands attention from the moment one sets foot through the garden gate. The array of plants evokes a feeling that each garden builder has a communion with nature. But what else would one expect from a people whose entire gardening tradition has been nature oriented.

From earliest times, the Japanese have been on intimate terms with their natural landscape both from a philosophical and practical viewpoint. That relationship was intensified by some 230 years of seclusion from about 1636 to 1868. During that era, the Japanese applied several centuries of Chinese influence to their own rich flora and added a devotion to detail that, in the case of garden design, produced some remarkable results.

From scores of wild plants, hundreds of improved varieties were selected and described and, in the instance of azaleas, over 300 selections appear in the *Kinshu*

JOHN L. CREECH, PH. D., *retired director of U.S. National Arboretum, currently consults, lectures and writes. He has conducted five plant collecting trips to Japan and has led several tours. He is an authority on Japanese plants and the history of Japanese horticulture. He is the co-author of* **A Brocade Pillow**, *a translation of the first book written on azaleas by Ito Ihei, 1692.*

Makura — the first book written on this popular garden plant in 1692. In 1845, a samurai, Matsudaira Sakinko, wrote the first basic book on *Hana Shobu (Iris kaempferi)*. He discussed how he found his first seedlings in the mountains near Fukushima (probably the Adzuma mountains), and he described details of culture, fertilization, how to raise seedlings and control beetle damage to the flowers.

Hundreds of books on the ennobling of wild ornamental species appeared during this period. Some are simple discussions of single plants, others are practical guides to the culture of flowering plants, and still others are complete encyclopedias, such as one with 96 volumes covering a range of subjects from medicinal plants, poisonous plants (azaleas are included here), and economic plants to ornamental and forestry species. Books on bonsai and flower arrangement were common as were those discussing how to use plants, stones and water in the garden.

It is no accident the Japanese were drawn to their wilderness. The mountainous terrain demanded that crop production areas be close to the forest, and farmers drew upon these natural

Ritsurin Park, Takamatsu, Japan Photo by George Taloumis

resources for fuel, timber, medicine and food supplements. Gradually planted forests displaced natural stands and *sugi* (*Cryptomeria japonica*) occupied the lower and more favorable sites while hinoki cypress (*Chamaecyparis obtusa*) was planted on higher and drier locations. The change was so gradual that probably little of the native flora was permanently displaced as a walk in an old *sugi* forest will show. In addition, shrine and temple forests tended to rely on the natural stands of trees and afforded protection to other plant life. Giant bamboos, introduced from China at an early era, appeared in the company of the native tree species to form a close knit support system for the farming population. As they worked in the forests or climbed the volcanic peaks in search of religious truths, the highly observant people collected attractive and unusual forms of flowering plants to enhance their tem-

ples, shrines and gardens. Being equally adventuresome businessmen, many farmers began to grow seedling trees and shrubs to replenish the forests and to provide plants for the feudal nobility who were engaged in beautifying their castle grounds. For example, when Edo (Tokyo) was destroyed by fire in 1657, the Shogun decreed that there be a massive tree and shrub planting program to revitalize the city. Many farmers around Kawaguchi and Angyo, just north of the city, became engaged in the nursery business to meet this demand for plants and thus began the famous nursery center which exists today.

These opportunities came about partly as a result of Japan's exceedingly rich flora of over 5,000 species of higher plants and the fact that broadleaved evergreens and conifers are major components of this flora. These are distinguished through a range of natural landscapes, from exquisite coastal barrens with windswept pines, a mixture of broadleaved trees and shrubs, and carpets of junipers, to rugged mountain panoramas with grand associations of azaleas, camellias and hollies which draw vast audiences of viewers.

The Japanese are so infatuated with these scenes that ship captains pass close to small islands in the Inland Sea so passengers may enjoy an appropriate view. But the variation is endless and no matter how many times one makes the journey to Japan, new adventures into the world of plants are in store.

Knowing about the natural landscapes of Japan is an aid to appreciating the Japanese garden, since native species have been used almost exclusively in their development.

Origin of Japan

According to legend, the islands of Japan were derived from the activities of the Gods who enjoyed life in the Plain of High Heaven, among whom were Izanagi and Izanami, husband and wife. Among his many heroic gestures, Izanagi once threw his jeweled spear into the deep and as he withdrew it, a shower of brilliant drops fell from the spear to become the verdant dragon-shaped island group we call Japan.

Instead of showering down, the islands were thrust up from the Pacific Basin as the peaks of submarine mountains that arose over a period of 60 million years from one of the deepest trenches in any ocean basin, with depths reaching 30,000 feet. In an unstable region, Japan experiences numerous volcanic eruptions and earthquakes.

Because of this dramatic origin, Japan is immensely rugged, consisting of over 75% mountains and hills with steep slopes. Although the mountains are not especially high (Mt. Fuji being the highest at 12,461 ft.) there are dozens of

mountains above 10,000 feet elevation, especially in the Japan Alps. These mountains are covered with luxurious forests and this green mantle is one of the lasting impressions of Japan. Because of Japan's unique geography, as an island chain running somewhat north-south-west off the coast of Asia, a moderate climate with ample rainfall prevails and the cool mountains contain a high proportion of broadleaved evergreens, trees, shrubs and groundcovers. Therefore all of the main elements essential to the Japanese landscape garden were readily available and in combinations that were often copied by the garden builders.

Wilderness Areas

The main sources of landscape materials are now preserved in the modern national park system of Japan and it is there one finds the natural landscape beauty reflected in gardens. There are 19 national parks and an additional 20 prefectural, or quasi-national parks, and 3 national gardens, the latter being the Imperial Palace Outer Garden, Shinjuku Gyoen and Kyoto Gyoen.

A trip to some of these areas will provide the gardener and traveler alike with background and ideas. The range of plant materials, outstanding landscapes, mountains and rocky coastlines seem endless. Visits to forests will reveal many remarkably fine plants not necessarily used in Japanese gardens and yet of interest. Beach areas are often covered with daylily species blooming in the summer. But the evergreen aspect of warmer Japan is gone.

There are so many treasure spots in Japan that many trips are essential to complete the story and witness the beauty of the four seasons as they relate to the Japanese garden. Fortunately the conservation system in Japan and the extent of these natural treasures assures that they will exist for a long time. 🌰

RECOMMENDED PLANTS FOR JAPANESE GARDENS IN AMERICA

STEPHEN A. MORRELL

Listed below are plants that are native to Asia and North America with an emphasis on Northeast Asia and eastern North America, as these two temperate floras are very similar with many identical species and related counterparts.

Using native plants of your area in addition to Japanese plants as a blending of two harmonious floras is in keeping with Japanese garden ideals.

This list is certainly not all-inclusive; varieties and cultivars are endless. In all cases a plant's hardiness rating should be considered for your area, as well as other cultural requirements.

EVERGREEN GROUNDCOVERS	COMMON NAME	COMMENTS—NATIVITY
Arctostaphylos uva-ursi	Bearberry	Eur., N. Asia, N. Amer.
Asarum shuttleworthii 'Callaway'	Wild ginger	SE U.S.
Galax urceolata	Wandflower	SE U.S.
Leucobryum glaucum	Cushion moss	Circumboreal
Liriope muscari	Lilyturf	Japan, China; numerous cultivars
Pachysandra terminalis	Japanese spurge	Japan; P. procumbens is an American counterpart
Polytrichum commune	Hairycap moss	Circumboreal
Sarcococca hookerana var. humilis	Sweet box	China
DECIDUOUS GROUNDCOVERS		
Hosta lancifolia	Narrow-leaved plantain lily	Japan
Hosta plantaginea	Fragrant plantain lily	Japan
Hosta sieboldiana	Plantain lily	Japan
Maianthemum canadense	Canada mayflower	Canada S to IN & W to NY; a Japanese mayflower is M. dilatatum.

Evergreen Groundcovers	Common Name	Comments—Nativity
Petasites japonicus	Fuki	Korea, China, Japan; petioles are eaten as a vegetable in Japan

Perennials

Anemone x hybrida	Japanese anemone	Japan, China
Arisaema triphyllum	Jack-in-the-pulpit	Many Japanese counterparts
Equisetum hyemale	Horsetail	Eurasia, Pacific N. Amer.
Erythronium americanum	Dogtooth violet	American counterpart to Japan's *E. dens-canis*
Iris cristata	Crested iris	SE U.S.
Iris kaempferi	Japanese iris	Japan; numerous cultivars
Iris pseudacorus	Yellow flag	W. Eur., N. Afr.; naturalized in N. Amer.
Polygonatum biflorum	Solomon's seal	N. Amer.
Polygonatum odoratum	Solomon's seal	Japan
Rodgersia aesculifolia	Bronzeleaf	China
Trillium erectum	Purple trillium	Many Japanese counterparts.

Ferns

Adiantum pedatum	Maidenhair fern	N. Amer. & E. Asia
Athyrium felix-femina	Lady fern	Temperate Northern Hemisphere
Athyrium goeringianum	Japanese painted fern	Japan
Dryopteris erythrosorus	Japanese shield fern	China, Japan; *D. marginalis* is an American counterpart
Polypodium virginianum	Rock polypody	E. N. Amer.
Polystichum acrostichoides	Christmas fern	E. N. Amer.

Bamboo & Ornamental Grasses

Arundinaria pygmaea	Kenezasa	Japan
Arundinaria variegata		
Arundinaria viridi-striata		
Sasa veitchii	Kumazasa	Japan — popular in gardens.
Sasa palmata		Japan, Sakhalin
Shibataea kumasaca	Okame-zasa	Japan — common in gardens.
Phyllostachys aureosulcata	Yellow groove bamboo	China
Phyllostachys nuda		China
Sinarundinaria nitida	Fountain bamboo	China
Thamnocalamus spathaceus	Umbrella bamboo	China

Evergreen Groundcovers	Common Name	Comments—Nativity
Miscanthus sinensis 'Gracillimus' 'Strictus'	Susuki	E. Asia, naturalized in some E. states
Pennisetum alopecuroides	Fountain grass	Asia

Aquatics

Nelumbo nucifera	Lotus	Orient; edible rhizomes & seeds; sacred to Buddhists.
Nymphaea sp.	Water lilies	Use hardy types

Vines

Hydrangea anomala subsp. *petiolaris*	Climbing hydrangea	Japan, Taiwan
Parthenocissus tricuspidata	Boston ivy	Central China, Japan
Wisteria floribunda	Japanese wisteria	Japan

Evergreen Shrubs

Abelia x grandiflora	Glossy abelia	China; semi-evergreen
Buxus microphylla	Littleleaf box	Japan
Camellia japonica	Camellia, Tsubaki	Japan; S. Korea, Taiwan
Cryptomeria japonica 'Elegans Nana'		A dwarf cultivar of this tree
Ilex crenata 'Helleri'		
Ilex x meserveae		
Ilex pedunculosa	Longstalk holly	Japan
Juniperus spp.	Juniper	Many species & cultivars are appropriate
Kalmia latifolia	Mountain laurel	E. N. Amer.
Leucothoe sp.		*L. fontanesiana* is a SE U.S. native
Mahonia bealei	Leatherleaf mahonia	Confused in cultivation with *M. japonica*, a Chinese species cultivated in Japan.
Photinia glabra	Japanese photinia	Japan
Picea abies 'Nidiformis'	Dwarf Norway spruce	Low with a dense head
Pieris japonica	Japanese pieris	Japan
Pinus strobus 'Nana'	Dwarf white pine	
Rhododendron keiskei		Central Japan
Rhododendron makinoi		Japan
Rhododendron obtusum	Kurume azalea	Japan; numerous cultivars
Rhododendron smirnowii		Caucasus

EVERGREEN GROUNDCOVERS	COMMON NAME	COMMENTS—NATIVITY
Rhododendron yakusimanum		Japan
Skimmia japonica	Japanese skimmia	Japan
Taxus baccata 'Repandens'	Weeping English yew	
Tsuga canadensis 'Pendula'	Weeping Canada hemlock	

DECIDUOUS SHRUBS

Acer palmatum var. *dissectum*	Cutleaf maple	Japan ; numerous cultivars
Berberis thunbergii		
'Crimson Pygmy'	Dwarf Japanese barberry	Japan
Callicarpa japonica	Japanese beautyberry	Japan, China
Clethra barbinervis	Japanese clethra	Japan; *C. alnifolia* is an American counterpart
Corylopsis pauciflora	Buttercup winterhazel	Japan
Corylus avellana 'Contorta'	Harry Lauder's walking stick	Europe
Cotinus coggygria	Smokebush	S Eur. to Asia
Cotoneaster horizontalis	Rockspray	W. China
Enkianthus perulatus		Japan
Ilex verticillata	Winterberry	N. Amer.
Lespedeza bicolor	Bush clover	Japan
Nandina domestica	Heavenly bamboo	India to E. Asia
Paeonia suffruticosa	Tree peony	China, Bhutan to Tibet; many cultivars
Rhododendron mucronatum	Snow azalea	Japan
Rhododendron schlippenbachii	Royal azalea	Manchuria, Korea, Japan
Viburnum plicatum var. *tomentosum*	Doublefile viburnum	China, Japan

DECIDUOUS LARGE SHRUBS-SMALL TREES

Acer griseum	Paperbark maple	China
Acer palmatum	Japanese maple	Korea, China, Japan
Amelanchier canadensis	Shadblow	Quebec to GA
Cornus kousa	Japanese dogwood	Japan, Korea
Cornus mas	Cornelian dogwood	Eur., W. Asia
Davidia involucrata var. *vilminiana*	Dove tree	W. China
Hamamelis mollis	Chinese witchhazel	W. China; American counterpart: *H. virginiana.*
Magnolia stellata	Star magnolia	Japan

Evergreen Groundcovers	Common Name	Comments—Nativity
Magnolia x loebneri 'Merrill'	Loebner magnolia	
Prunus maackii		E. Asia
Prunus mume	Japanese apricot	E Asia
Prunus serrulata	Japanese flowering cherry	E Asia
Prunus subhirtella 'Pendula'	Weeping Higan cherry	Japan
Oxydendrum arboreum	Sourwood	PA to IL, S to FL
Salix matsudana 'Tortuosa'	Corkscrew willow	
Stewartia pseudocamellia	Japanese stewartia	Japan; American counterparts: *S. ovata & S. malacodendron*
Styrax japonicus	Japanese snowbell	Japan, China; American counterparts: *S. grandifolius & S. americanus*
Viburnum sieboldii	Siebold viburnum	Japan

Evergreen Trees

Chamaecyparis obtusa	Hinoki false cypress	Japan; numerous cultivars
Cryptomeria japonica	Japanese cedar, Sugi	Japan; numerous cultivars
Ilex opaca	American holly	N. Amer.
Ilex pendunculosa	Longstalk holly	China, Japan
Pinus bungeana	Lace-bark pine	NW China
Pinus densiflora' Umbraculifera'	Tanyosho pine	Japan
Pinus koraiensis	Korean pine	Japan, Korea
Pinus parviflora	Japanese white pine	Japan
Pinus strobus	White pine	N. Amer.; various dwarf cultivars
Pinus sylvestris	Scotch pine	Eurasia
Pinus thunbergiana	Japanese black pine	Japan
Sciadopitys verticillata	Japanese umbrella pine	SW Japan

Deciduous Trees

Acer rubrum	Red maple	U.S.
Cercidiphyllum japonicum	Katsura tree	Japan, China
Ginkgo biloba	Maidenhair tree	Frequently seen at temples in Japan
Koelreuteria paniculata	Goldenrain tree	China, Korea, & naturalized in Japan
Metasequoia glyptostroboides	Dawn redwood	China
Nyssa sylvatica	Sourgum, tupelo	E. N. Amer.
Prunus yedoensis	Yoshino cherry	In cultivation in Japan; unknown in the wild.

MOSS GARDENING

Michael B. Trimble

Growing moss ornamentally is not a widely accepted practice in American gardens. Unstinting efforts and considerable sums of money are spent annually to eradicate these diminutive plants. Sadly, we have come to automatically equate the presence of moss with horticultural inadequacy in the garden. Persuading fellow gardeners to reconsider the ornamental potential these plants embody is a challenge.

Mosses, along with lichens, were among the first plants to establish themselves upon the barren rock of the early land masses left in the wake of receding oceans, but their ability to grow where little else will, while worthy of our admiration, has instead earned them a reputation as weeds. Favoring spots where shade and dampness thwart the growth of grasses and flowering plants, the presence of moss is taken as an indication that such spots are culturally deficient, further adding to our tendency to regard them as undesirable garden inhabitants.

How differently we look upon the mosses in nature that cluster at the bases of trees in a shady woods, or cling tenaciously to the rocky faces of boulders.

MICHAEL B. TRIMBLE *is a landscape gardener and horticultural writer in Rhinebeck, NY. His articles have appeared in* **American Horticulturist.**

Frequently mosses and lichens will share a rocky cleft or moist recess among the roots of an old tree, their varied shapes and colors providing a visual feast to the observant. The lush, moist greens, grays and even whites of a moss-strewn stream bank or moist woodland floor evoke an appreciative response—mosses are certainly not weeds! In their native habitats they personify the gentler, more pacific side of our natural surroundings. They contrast with the rugged character of rocky crags and mountain tops, the dignity of mature trees, and blend with the fluid energy of streams and cascades. In their natural settings mosses please the eye without rousing feelings of disdain.

In Japan, nature has been the guide in the creation of both public and private, religious and secular gardens. Replication is rarely the aim; instilling some feeling of the spectacular natural beauty of Japanese islands within the garden is the goal. Mosses' serene character and ability to blend harmoniously with rock, water and plants used in creating a garden have earned them favored status among Japanese gardeners. Looking upon an expanse of moss as it runs in among the roots of trees or up to the rocky edge of a stream or waterfall, one can easily appreciate the ornamental usefulness of these agreeable little plants.

Moss Botany

Mosses lack true roots and vascular tissues which trees, shrubs and flowering plants possess. Instead they have primitive, rootlike structures called rhizoids which anchor a moss plant to its chosen home, while the task of taking up moisture is shared by nearly all surfaces of a moss that come in contact with water.

Mosses also differ from most garden plants by their reproductive cycle. Taking the hairycap moss, *Polytrichum commune,* as an example, the soft green carpets of small plants we recognize as moss are made up of sexual, or gametophytic representatives of species. Each individual will spawn both male and female gametes. The gametes meet and fuse if the moss is cloaked in sufficient moisture for the male gamete to move from its point of origin to where the female gamete is formed. This assures the development for the alternate, sporophytic generation.

The sporophytic, or asexual genera-tion, is represented by a spore producing capsule normally on a stalk that remains attached to the gametophytic parent. From the spore produced in the capsule, the next gametophytic generation will germinate, which we again recognize as moss. This means of achieving sexual reproduction is surprisingly efficient, belying their apparent vulnerability.

Botanists have identified upwards of 14,000 species of moss, with species adapted to such varied habitats as moist and shady, dry and sunny, soil dwellers, wood dwellers and those that prefer solid rock. Most are easily grown. However, to grow them well one must take the time to match a given species to its desired growing conditions.

Most mosses likely to be used in the garden thrive where soils are moist year round, shade is plentiful during the summer and the soil is acidic. Mosses found growing on wood or stone can be used as well, with best results coming when the mosses and their chosen home are

A bed of moss in a raked dry garden.

Moss growing between the rocks in Nanzenji Garden, Kyoto, Japan.

PHOTO BY ELIZABETH SCHOLTZ

moved together into the garden.

Mosses are tough. They can suspend their growth processes, entering a state of dormancy, when the conditions of their environment do not favor continued growth. Severe cold, heat, or drought can all be endured.

If suitable shade and moisture are available, mosses can be used in many spots where lawn grasses fail and herbaceous groundcovers can't get established. Mosses are an excellent contrast to both stone and wood and can be used advantageously in shady rockeries or to cloak the ground left bare by the greedy roots of shallow rooted shade trees. Their tendency to go dormant as their surroundings dry can be off-set with an occasional watering. Having no true roots, such waterings need not be deep.

Moss lawns are becoming popular where excessive shade thwarts the use of lawn grasses. A close look at your own lawn will probably reveal a wealth of mosses intermingled with the grasses where trees cast their shade.

If hairycaps dominate the mosses already present, steps to acidify the soil may be all that is needed to encourage their dominance of the entire area. Dusting with sulfur to lower the soil's pH to a level of 6.0 or less will usually do the trick. Weeds less finicky about pH must be removed manually.

Simple steps are needed to introduce mosses into a garden. First, be sure the site offers growing conditions that will foster their vigorous growth. Secondly, prepare the site by removing all non-moss growth that might interfere with

33

their later care and appearance. Lichens, ferns and wildflowers all belong to the group of plants I would leave in place while grasses and groundcovers such as pachysandra and ivy should be removed. Mosses do not need fertile soil and its presence often hinders moss by encouraging the growth of weeds. Good moisture retention is desirable and steps to improve a soil's tilth will benefit a moss planting over the long run.

The most straightforward way to bring mosses into the garden is to transplant moss sods. The usual source will be colonies growing wild which will provide the opportunity to observe their growing conditions first hand. Emulating their preference will help assure success in the garden. In Japan, moss sods can be purchased much like turf.

When collecting mosses from the wild take only what is needed and leave as much as possible undisturbed to insure that the native colonies will continue to prosper. Mosses are tough and can re-establish themselves quickly, however, excessive collecting can imperil both the diversity and vitality of native moss colonies, especially those growing in exposed locations.

With the sods in hand and their new home properly prepared, moisten the sod and planting area and set the sod firmly in place. Given ample moisture, the moss' rhizoids will readily anchor the sod and the colony will slowly begin to expand outward. The cool days of spring and autumn are best suited to moss transplanting. In addition, the absence of tall grasses and other herbaceous plants at these times will make it easier to spot the mosses you want.

Mosses can also be introduced by means of spores. However, this is a more labor-intensive method and less reliable as it gives weeds a better chance to move in before the mosses do.

Mosses are also capable of regenerat-ing themselves from bits and pieces dislodged from an actively growing or dormant plant. Gather pieces of moss, dry them and then spread the powdered bits over moist soil. This method has the drawback of leaving the young plants vulnerable to weeds and weather. However, it can be a useful means for getting moss to grow in tight spots where it is difficult to anchor sods.

The care of moss planting involves little more than 1) watering when needed, 2) weeding, and 3) keeping leaves off the moss in winter. In Japan, expanses of moss are swept regularly while the maritime climate can usually be relied upon to keep them well watered.

Recommended Species

The most popular and perhaps the best moss for covering large areas is the hairycap, *Polytrichum commune*. Its dark green tint and soft, needlelike appearance offers a most appealing substitute for grass. Its uniform height never needs mowing, insects and diseases are no problem and most weeds can be discouraged by acidifying the soil.

The common fern moss, *Thuidium delicatulum* is another splendid addition to a moss planting. Its delicate, light green, featherlike form is effective at the base of gnarled roots or skirting in among a grouping of lichen-encrusted stone. The greenish-white tufts of the pincushion moss, *Leucobryum glaucum*, are a useful contrast while the windswept appearance of the broom mosses, *Dicranus* spp., make fine additions to the garden. The happy-to-grow-just-about-anywhere cord moss, *Funaria hygrometrica*, will readily fill in where needed.

The beauty we see in them in their native settings can be transferred into the garden through careful attention to garden design and site preparation, with the gardens of Japan serving as vivid examples of how it can be done. ❧

BAMBOOS AND JAPANESE GARDENING

KIM SORVIG

There are bamboos
ten thousand meters high
if you look at their shadows by moonlight.

Su Tung-P'o (1037-1101,
China, Sung dynasty)

Bamboo is a state of mind. To use it effectively in a garden, especially a Japanese garden, it is not enough to know how to grow it. That is in many ways *less* important than having a feel for bamboo's history, evocative power and cultural import. Bamboos have long shadows indeed, for they are the most useful group of plants known to humankind and are as mysterious and mystical as any living thing on earth. Whether cast by the moonlight of intuition or the stark light of scientific study, a sense of these ten-thousand-meter shadows help give bamboo its proper place in a garden.

There are excellent Japanese gardens which lack a single *living* bamboo, but even in the stone garden of Ryoanji, there are elements *crafted* of bamboo. In fact, in Japan and China, bamboo is so much a part of the fabric of life, it seems there would hardly have *been* any Oriental culture to give birth to such gardens, without the influence of the giant grasses.

The Kingdom of Bamboo

Bamboos are a large subfamily of the grasses, woody and often giant. Their natural range centers in Asia, ('bamboo' is a Malay word), but includes Africa and the Americas. They range in size from 100-foot-tall giants to tiny ground-creepers, and grow in habitats from jungle riverbank to the high Himalayas. About 45 genera have been named, making several hundred species.

Mysteries surround the bamboos, and one need not be a botanist to experience this. Very little can equal the radiantly dim light inside a bamboo forest, the subtle colors from waxy white through yellow, green, to purple and black, the

KIM SORVIG *is in the Department of Landscape Architecture & Regional Planning at the University of Pennsylvania, Philadelphia. He holds the Diploma in Horticulture from the Royal Botanic Gardens, Kew, in London and he also does freelance design and consulting.*

graceful columnar stems, and the sound of leaves rustling in the air and underfoot. Flexible yet indomitable, it is small wonder that bamboo is one of the three plants (with pine and plum) that symbolize the essential virtues in Japan. Even a small planting has something magnetic about it.

Besides inspiring wonder in lay people, bamboos almost seem to *exist* to confound botanists! These "trees" are actually grasses, their "culms" (stems) hollow and segmented by "nodes" or joints, at which branching occurs. They are woody, but do *not* grow by annual rings. Their evolutionary history remains a conundrum: while their modern center of distribution is Asia, recent studies indicate that their nearest living relatives may be small, non-woody grasses now known mainly in the New World. Ecological jacks-of-all-trades, they adopt almost every kind of survival strategy, as canopy, understory, shrub, ground layer, or even vine; few plant families show such wide adaptability. This great diversity of form is unusual in a group whose reproduction is normally *vegetative;* besides, their chromosomes show *little* variability! As for their flowering, it is a subject for both botanical and mythological research!

Evolutionary relics themselves, the giant pandas have a particular interest in bamboo's flowering, as do gardeners. Many bamboos grow for 30-120 years before ever flowering. Some flower once and die. There have been reports that these cycles are synchronized for every bamboo of a species, even when transplanted continents from "home." *Some* of this is possibly myth; it is definitely not true for all species. Many garden specimens are clones of a single parent, which may explain some cases of synchronous flowering. But the mystery, and the consternation it causes, remains.

For a plant competing in an ecosystem, either fast growth or the strength and height provided by woodiness can help. But it is a rare plant that can do *both:* only very soft tissue can grow fast, but soft stems cannot reach great heights. The bamboos have solved this paradox rather neatly. The solution? A tight "sheath," a leaflike structure which wraps around each growing segment of the culm so tightly that it can *only* grow upwards. And grow they do: some species up to 40 inches a day, fast enough to stand and watch. Once the culm stops growing, becomes woody, and can support itself, the culm-sheath drops away. The side-groove typical of bamboo stems is formed by 'extrusion' as the culm pushes past a branch-bud held tightly in place by the sheath.

Traditional Garden Uses of Bamboo

The many uses of bamboo in traditional Oriental gardens reflect its ecological diversity. Trees, shrubs, or groundcover: bamboo fills many niches, in design as in nature.

The larger bamboos make wonderful forests, 100 feet tall and covering many acres, with little undergrowth and an open, lively feeling which suggests the interior of Japanese houses. In the largest palace gardens, such forests divide or frame whole landscapes, and form groves through which to walk among the foot-thick jointed stems (culms).

Medium-size bamboos (10-50 feet) are far more common in U.S. gardens. These can form screens or stand alone as featured plantings. They are also used as understory with deciduous canopy trees (but not with the larger bamboos). Being mostly evergreen, they are useful as a backdrop and for winter interest. Their vertical culms make a striking accent, especially effective in tiny courtyards or reflected in water.

The small bamboos serve as shrub-

Bamboo can be used as a construction material, as it is in this hand-tied fence.

bery, groundcover and hedges, often clipped. They too have a variety of textures and are usually evergreen. Small and medium-sized species can be planted as half-hardy perennials in colder zones, and also grown in containers.

The textural variety of bamboo finds great expression in Japanese gardens. Their form may be upright or arching, with few or many branches, straight or zig-zag; leaf size, shape, density, and color vary; the new sheaths are tufted, finely hairy, ribbed or smooth. There are a number of "abnormal" forms, such as the Tortoise-shell and Buddha's-belly bamboos, in which the internodes swell and contort into fantastic shapes. Almost every color except bright red can be found among bamboos which are sometimes striped or spotted.

Without bamboo as construction material, the gardens of the East would be much impoverished. Fences of whole or split canes, woven or tied or pegged, trip-rails of bent split canes, posts, gates,

handles—all are common, in hundreds of designs. Bamboo can be steamed and bent into almost any shape. It is often inserted into plaster walls to frame or divide an opening.

Two very traditional Japanese constructions for the garden are the *tsukubai* water basin, and the *shishi-odoshi* or "deer-scarer." The *tsukubai* may be fed through a bamboo pipe musically dripping water and include a bamboo scoop for drinking or washing. The water scarecrow is always made of bamboo constructed from a large culm, set on a pivot and driven by water. It makes a resonant, eerie booming sound that echoes through the garden.

Cultivating the Bamboo

All bamboos grow from rhizomes; from buds on these grow the culms (also called 'canes,' a term better reserved for dried bamboo). Each culm gains full height and diameter in ONE season, unlike trees. It will harden, still alive, for

37

Shishi-odoshi
(Deer-scarer)

 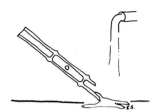 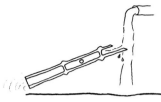

| 1. Bamboo two-and-one half nodes long, on a pivot; the short end fills with water and drops. | 2. Water spills out and the long end is once again heaviest. | 3. Long end falls, strikes the ground and resonates. Water refills the short end. |

several years, and if not harvested will die standing.

Based on the way their rhizomes spread, bamboos are classed as "clump-forming" or "running," an *extremely important* distinction when selecting them for a site.

CLUMP bamboos tend to form dense, slow-spreading stands with culms close together. Their rhizomes are rather short and stout. Mainly of tropical origin, they shoot when rains follow a dry season, usually in summer or early autumn in the US. Few are frost hardy. *Bambusa* and *Dendrocalamus* are main clump genera grown.

RUNNING bamboos tend to have long, slender rhizomes, resulting in a more open stand and more invasive habits. Represented by *Phyllostachys, Sasa*, and *Arundinaria*, they are native to temperate climates, and therefore sprout in response to spring warmth. They are relatively hardy, and few are happy in year-round warmth.

Two misconceptions about bamboo are common causes of problems: one, that they are all heat-loving, and two, that they like swampy soils. There are bamboos hardy to — 20 degrees F, and wind- and sun-scorch strongly affect hardiness. And they will NOT tolerate waterlogging, which suffocates and rots the rhizomes. Excellent drainage is probably more important than plentiful water, though that is usually needed too.

Selecting Bamboo Species

AVAILABILITY: Bamboos are usually sold as container nursery stock. The American Bamboo Society (ABS) compiles an updated list, at present showing 95 species and 22 suppliers in the USA. The list is free for a self-addressed stamped

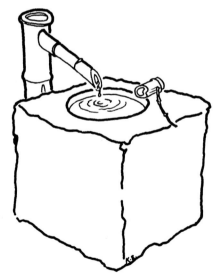

Tsukubai with bamboo plumbing and water scoop or ladle. There are many types of water basins. This one has a hidden faucet connection to allow a constant water source.

envelope. Importing bamboos could bring in grass-family diseases that endanger major cereal crops and is prohibited by quarantine regulations.

ON NAMING: One problem in obtaining bamboo is the jumble of names by which they are known. Many species have no common name in English. Flowers, on which scientific names are based, have rarely been observed, in some species never, so experts disagree on Latin names. Nurserymen and collectors are understandably confused so everyone adopts some compromise. In this article, the names used in the ABS list are followed for convenience.

HARDINESS: In general, the true clump bamboos are injured or killed by 0 degree F, some by 5 degrees; a few can take —10 degrees. The running bamboo will survive between 0 and — 10 degrees on average. Rhizomes may survive much colder winters than culms, and sprout anew each year, as half-hardy plantings.

Where hardiness is crucial, *Phyllostachys nuda, P. flexuosa, P. aureosulcata,* *Sinarundinaria nitida, Pseudosasa japonica* and the *Sasas* are most reliable.

Invaders: These species are particularly invasive and should always be contained unless space is unlimited: *Arundinaria anceps, A. vagans, A. pygmaea, A. variegata, A. viridistriata; Sasas,* especially *S. palmata;* under good conditions *Pseudosasa japonica;* and most *Phyllostachys* given time, though less so than the above.

SUBSTITUTES & IMPOSTERS: "Sacred-, heavenly-, or Flowering-bamboo," *Nandina domestica,* is a Chinese relative of barberry, not a bamboo. Its foliage is vaguely bamboolike, attractive as a substitute or in its own right.

Many reeds, pampas, grasses, etc. (including *Arundo,* not to be confused with *Arundinaria*) can give bamboolike effects in areas where bamboos cannot grow.

"Mexican Bamboo" is *Polygonum cuspidatum.* This extremely invasive weed should only be considered as a bamboo substitute in very harsh climates; elsewhere it is uncontainable. It does

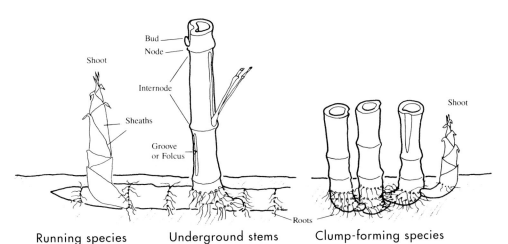

Running species Underground stems Clump-forming species

All bamboos grow from rhizomes, and from buds on these grow the culms (also called canes) which are jointed above-ground stems. Each culm gains full height and diameter in one season. Pictured above are the two types of bamboos based on the way their rhizomes spread.

DRAWINGS COURTESY OF THE AUTHOR

resemble a 3-8 foot bamboo at first glance, but it is related to buckwheat. "Mexican Weeping Bamboo," however, is a true bamboo, *Otatea aztecorum*.

Establishment, Care and Problems

PLANTING AND ROUTINE CARE: Select or create a well-drained, moist location, fertile and sheltered from strong wind — the smaller the species, the more shade, as a rule of thumb. Drainage is essential and poor drainage should be improved to the depth of 18-24 inches by adding gravel to subsoil and sand to topsoil. The water table should be at least 18 inches below the surface. High nitrogen fertilizer is beneficial. Build containment structures if needed.

For even stands, bamboos should be spaced at about half their mature height. Refirm the soil. Planting depth should match the old soil mark (there will be a color change on younger culms); usually, this buries the main rhizomes two-four inches. Water until soil is settled (tamping can damage rhizomes). Apply mulch to a depth of two-three inches.

For the first season, watering is critical. The soil should never dry; a thorough one inch water every 5-10 days minimum is needed. Once established, bamboos are quite tough. Little care is needed except yearly fertilization and mulching just before shoots appear and irrigation if climate dictates. Dead culms should be removed or they choke the clump. Pruning all three-year-old culms gives maximum regrowth for most species while taking only four-five year ones promotes fewer but larger culms.

TRANSPLANTING BAMBOO: The commonest method of propagating bamboo of all species is by divisions transplanted in the spring. Divisions may be taken from the edge of a clump, or the whole clump dug up and split. The smallest division should include two culms (from two years' previous growth), connected by rhizomes and showing a strong new shoot-bud. Usually it is wise to take larger divisions, about a foot square. The fibrous roots may keep a division with dead or missing rhizomes alive for several seasons, but new shoots will not be reproduced.

Bamboo transplants' roots and foliage are *very* vulnerable to drying. The transplanted culms will most likely die within one or two seasons, by which time there will be new culms to carry on. To slow transpiration when dividing, the old culms can be cut back. But opinions vary on whether this should be done or not. Cut-back culms are unsightly and the process deprives new shoots of shade and shelter which can be critical. Pruning a number of whole *branches* seems preferable; antitranspirants might also be justified. Painstaking moisture protection can allow division at any time *except* when new culms are extending rapidly.

PHYSICAL DAMAGE: Rhizomes lie near the surface. Cultivating tools, tamping during planting, and careless walking can damage them. Wind whipping older culms can kill or deform soft new shoots. Tying five or six culms together in a "tipi" will prevent snow damage and mulch will increase frost tolerance.

PESTS & DISEASES: There are few and are mostly confined to hot humid areas. Rust fungus causes leaf spots and if removing diseased leaves is not enough, fungicides may be used.

Scale insects are common but only unsightly on California and Florida bamboos: they can be removed with soap or oil spray. Mealybug can be removed by water pressure. Ants usually 'herd' these insects, and may require control.

Squirrels and rabbits can be serious pests when their populations are large and hungry, as they eat bamboo shoots. The hard culms are not palatable to these animals, so temporary protection of soft shoots is practicable.

Bamboo "trees" are actually grasses. The larger bamboos make wonderful forests 100 feet tall, with little undergrowth and an open feeling which suggests the interior of Japanese houses.

PHOTO BY ELIZABETH SCHOLTZ

Lawn chemicals near bamboos should be watched with great care since as grasses, bamboos react differently to poisons than broad-leaf plants. Bamboos are vigorous enough to out-compete most weeds anyhow.

FLOWERING: This remains a vexed question for bamboo growers. Many species flower on a few culms each year and even those that flower and die will probably grow back from rhizomes or from seed. If prize specimens start to flower, some gardeners try heavy watering, large doses of nitrogen fertilizer and pruning the flowering branches. This may or may not help and should only be tried if flowering is noticed.

CONTAINMENT & ERADICATION: The most effective method of controlling invasive species is to put a solid curb around the planting. This should be 24-30 inches deep, extending an inch above soil. It can be made of concrete poured directly into a narrow trench of sheet metal, thick plastic lining or other material so long as all joints are lapped, tightly joined and sealed. Escape is likely through any hole 1/4 inch or larger!

Mowing or hand removal of all unwanted new shoots will contain bamboo with barriers, but requires vigilance. Trenching (or for dwarf species slicing with a spade) all around the stand may be effective if done annually. Don't forget the neighbor's yard — gardener and bamboo alike can get a very bad name! Bamboo rhizomes are unlikely to damage walks or foundations as they usually change directions first. If bamboo must be completely removed, dig it out or cut it down; remove any new shoots by hand by mowing or plowing.

Far from being rooted out, however, bamboos are useful, magical plants which can add to any garden, Japanese or not. 🍃

41

HEDGES: Most bamboos can be used for hedges and windbreaks. *Bambusa glaucescens* (a.k.a. *B. multiplex*) is called Hedge Bamboo; for clipped hedges it and *Shibataea kumasaca* are two of the best. *Sasa tesselata, S. palmata,* and *Arundinaria anceps* (all strictly contained), *A. simonii, Semiarundinaria fastuosa, Pseudosasa japonica, Sinarundinaria nitida, Thamnocalamus spathaceus,* and smaller *Physllostachys* such as *P. nigra* are also good choices.

For hedge use, choose a species whose mature height exceeds the desired hedge height by 25%. Plant closely (about one quarter the expected height). Running species must be contained in a trench, and their runners aligned with its length. Allow the planting to gain mature height (usually 3 years) before beginning to clip once or twice yearly. Thin older culms evenly and regularly.

CONTAINER PLANTING: The Japanese, rather than fight climate, make excellent use of indoor/outdoor container plants, changed seasonally. In addition to tender bamboos such as *Bambusa glaucescens, Arundinaria falconeri, A. aristata, A. hookeriana,* and *Sinobambusa tootsik,* several hardy species thrive in tubs, showing off their decorative culms. Among these are any *Chimonobambusa,* including the marbled *C. marmorea* and square-stemmed *C. quadrangularis; Phyllostachys aurea* with its swollen nodes, and *P. nigra's* dark stems. *Pseudosasa japonica, Sinarundinaria nitida,* and *Thamnocalamus spathaceus* are also attractive.

Potted bamboos must have coarse, well-drained soil, and regular feeding and watering. Liquid fertilizer twice weekly is needed during shooting; the soil must neither be dry nor be sodden; and humidity should be moderate, avoiding drafts. Bamboos like generous root space, but seem to regulate their own growth before becoming potbound; if repotting, root-prune at the base of the ball to avoid lifting in the pot. Night temperatures should be dropped to 45-50 degrees F in winter for temperate species, which do not thrive in year-round heat; tropical species require minimum temperatures 10-20 degrees degrees higher.

CANES: In an Oriental garden, bamboo timber is indispensable. It is simple to manage an ornamental planting to serve this second purpose. Some of the best species are *Arundinaria amabilis* (Tonkin cane), *A. anceps, A. simonii, Bambusa glaucescens, B. oldhamii, B. tulda, Phyllostachys bambusoides, P. meyeri, P. nigra, P. aurea, Pseudosasa japonica, Sinarundinaria nitida,* and *Chimonobambusa falcata.* Potassium and phosphorus fertilizer can increase strength.

The planting should be allowed to grow uncut for 3 years. For sustainable harvest, one year's growth must equal one year's cut; mark the new culms each year with paint. Harvest with a hacksaw when the culms start to turn yellowish tan. Cure in a dry, shady, ventilated place for 3-12 months; support to avoid warp, and turn periodically.

Properly cured, canes resist rot for 10 years. Lashing is best for joining them; pegs, nails, and bolts will work with pre-drilled holes. To split canes, use a sharp knife and even pressure from the *top*; a rod run through the membranes inside the nodes makes bamboo pipe. A node with one branch attached makes a water-scoop for the *tsukubai.*

SHOOTS: Western gardens are intimately connected with food, and a Japanese garden need not be a museum piece. Many ornamental bamboos provide that delicacy of Oriental cuisine, the edible shoot. *Phyllostachys dulcis, P. nidularia, P. mitis,* and *P. bambusoides* are among the sweetest; many others can be used if boiled in two waters.

To ensure sustained yield, the Japanese use this system, which also gives an annual harvest of canes: establish the planting for 3 years, or until mature-size culms are being produced. Mark *and count* the first set of full-size culms. Next Spring **LEAVE** that number of shoots to grow into culms, marking them with a new color, and harvest all other shoots to eat. Repeat every year, and as each group of marked culms reaches 5 years of age, harvest them in Fall for canes.

FOR FURTHER INFORMATION AND BAMBOO SOURCES CONTACT:
The American Bamboo Society
1101 San Leon Court • Solana Beach, CA. 92075 • (714) 481-9869

THE JAPANESE GARDEN OF THE BROOKLYN BOTANIC GARDEN

This garden in Brooklyn is a traditional Japanese landscape garden, designed and constructed in 1914-1915 by Mr. Takeo Shiota. It was his ambition to make the most beautiful garden in the world. By 1915 he had designed and constructed eight gardens in the vicinity of New York, and his crowning achievement was the one in Brooklyn. All lovers of beauty are indebted to this talented artist who came from Japan in 1907 and lived in New York until his death in 1946.

This garden centers upon a small lake, the outlines of which describe the strokes of the Chinese character *shin*, meaning 'heart' or 'mind.' The lake is fed by a cascade of waterfalls. A small turtle-shaped island is reached by a Drum Bridge. A roofed Waiting Pavilion faces the lake, and hanging out over the water is a modified Tea House with adjacent open pavilion.

In the largest section of the lake stands a *torii* or 'gateway to heaven.' The Shrine on the hill beyond is dedicated to Inari, the Shinto God of Harvest.

There is a tall pedestal-type stone lantern near the waterfall and a low, broad-roofed 'snow-viewing' lantern on the island.

The principal plants of Japanese origin that are included in this garden are Japanese maples, flowering cherries, azaleas, barberry and flowering quince. Restrained use is made of Japanese irises in small clumps around the lake. Flowering plants are used with restraint. ❧

Brooklyn Botanic Garden's own Hill-and-Pond Garden, shown here garbed in the colors of autumn, changes with the seasons.

The torii is modeled after the famous camphorwood one in Miyajima, which stands in the sea.

THE CHALLENGE OF BUILDING A JAPANESE GARDEN IN THE UNITED STATES

KOICHI KAWANA

Sansho-En, Chicago Botanic Garden's promenade-style garden on three islands, was designed by the author.

PHOTO BY KRIS JARANTOSKI

I n the period following the end of World War II, many "Japanese gardens" were built in the United States. However, most of them tended to be merely an assemblage of typically Jap-

KOICHI KAWANA, M.F.A., PH.D., *a native of Japan, is Principal Architectural Associate and lecturer in Japanese art, architecture and landscape design at the University of California, Los Angeles. He is also a partner of Environmental Design Association and has designed gardens throughout the U.S.*

anese features derived from books on Japanese gardens or copied from photographs of features in such gardens.

No garden should be constructed in a foreign environment without being closely related to its surroundings. The degree of authenticity of a Japanese garden depends, for the most part, on the creativity and the statement of the designer, as the basic principles of such a garden are assimilated to the unique local environment. This is a major challenge since the garden must be designed with local climatic and topographical limitations in mind.

According to the *Sakuteiki*, the earliest known Japanese garden manual compiled in the 11th century, a particular topography suggests or demands a certain kind of garden design and the designer should respond to it. The subordination of man relative to nature is a time-honored design concept in Japan.

Fortunately, I have had the opportunity to design Japanese gardens throughout the United States including ones in St. Louis, Chicago, Denver and Los Angeles. Most of these cities experience extreme seasonal variations in temperature and many trees and plants commonly used in gardens in Japan will not survive. For this reason, I worked closely with staff members of those gardens to search for plants which grow well in these climates and, at the same time, possess the shape and texture to recommend their use as substitutes for plants found in Japan.

Japanese black pines (*Pinus thunbergiana*) are featured trees in gardens in Japan and in that country, beautifully shaped pines have been readily available. But climatic conditions in some of the cities of the United States make it necessary to substitute Scotch, Austrian (*P. sylvestris, P. nigra*) or other pines. Bushy, untrained pines with the potential for training must be found. They must be trained to take on beautiful forms. Imagination, skill and patience are required. Difficulties are found with other plants which are typical for gardens in Japan such as camellias, azaleas, threadleaf Japanese maples, bamboo and moss, and substitutes must often be found for them as well.

The search for and selection of rocks and their proper arrangement poses another major challenge for the garden builder. The arranged rocks are the skeleton of the Japanese garden. In Japan, the designer can select stones ideal in shape and color at a stoneyard even though the cost may be substantial, but in the U.S. finding appropriate rocks and arranging for their transportation is difficult. It is often necessary to utilize poorly shaped stones to develop a stone arrangement.

Since the stone arrangement is the major structure in a Japanese garden, the designer in Japan may spend hours to set one stone or to change an arrangement found to be inappropriate. In the U.S. the contractor, conscious of the cost of time and labor, depends upon the designer to make a swift decision as to which is the top or bottom and front or back of the stone as it is lifted by a crane and hangs in the air. Once it is positioned, it is difficult to change it. Thus, in the United States, those involved in stone arrangements need additional skill and training to achieve the desired goals.

For a Western type landscape the designer creates a design and provides the landscape contractor with a blueprint. The latter installs trees and stones according to the drawings and specifications furnished. In building a Japanese garden, however, the blueprint serves only as a general guide and is useless unless the garden is constructed by the designer himself or by a garden technician who is familiar with Japanese installations. Otherwise the design may be excellent but the end product may be a disaster.

The arrangement of stones and feature trees can be compared to the creation of a sculpture especially when form, size and line movement are considered. In Japan, the designer or architect will either personally supervise the installation or delegate it to the *Niwashi* or garden technicians who specialize in stone arrangements and plantings in such gardens. In the United States, the designer of a Japanese garden needs to be an installer and should also possess expertise on the trimming and training of feature trees.

Another challenge to the builder of Japanese gardens in the U.S. is the difficulty encountered in meeting the requirements posed by local building codes. Such codes affect the building of the foundations of arbors and other garden structures, the materials and construction of teahouses and bridges and the treatment of the edges of lakes. These structures must be authentic in appearance, but many of the structural elements require the closest collaboration with engineers in order to pass the required government inspections.

The use of building materials such as bamboo, cedar bark and black rope poses another challenge. In Japan, materials of this type are replaced every several years. In the United States their use would be limited, durable substitutes should be found or, ideally, proper maintenance and cyclic replacement should be insured.

The element of time plays an important role in a Japanese garden. After Zen Buddhism became popular in Japan during the 13th to the 15th centuries, Zen esthetics such as *wabi, sabi, shibui, yugen* and *koko* which can be translated as "profound and refined elegance with the quality of aged maturity," became essential values for a Japanese garden. Such values can be achieved only by the passage of time accompanied by caring maintenance. For this reason the designing and building of a Japanese garden are only the beginning. To achieve maximum potential, the garden will require time and meticulous care. In this respect I have been called on to instruct the garden staff in maintenance procedures during the construction phase of many gardens and to make periodic visits to those gardens previously built in order to oversee their maintenance and development efforts.

It is ironic that, due to Westernization and funding problems, many of the difficulties which have faced those developing Japanese gardens in the U.S. now beset Japanese gardens in Japan. 🌿

THE JAPANESE GARDEN

AT THE DAWES ARBORETUM

NEWARK, OHIO

ALAN D. COOK

Some visitors to the Japanese Garden at the Dawes Arboretum are disappointed because of "plainness". Others are delighted, for the same reason. They see a garden designed to instill tranquility yet blend smoothly with the open fields and rolling hills of central Ohio.

The garden was designed and constructed by Makoto Nakamura, Lecturer in Landscape Architecture, University of Kyoto, Japan, during a cultural exchange visit in 1964.

Mr. Nakamura conceived the garden "as an experiment in the exchange of two cultures — American and Japanese." He points out that it can hardly be called an "authentic" Japanese garden because it is constructed of American materials by local craftsmen to suit American conditions. On the other hand it presents the basic idea of Japanese design which is to create landscapes suggested by natural scenery. In Mr. Nakamura's words, "In

ALAN D. COOK, *Director of Extended Services, The Dawes Aboretum, Newark, OH, has been guest editor of four Brooklyn Botanic Garden Handbooks and contributor to several others.*

the Japanese garden these are abstracted from real landscapes, but they are easily recognizable."

This garden is composed of two parts. One enters a lower-level where there are several earth mounds capped by rugged boulders, and a "dry run" bordered with rocks. Mr. Nakamura writes, "the motif here is a forceful landscape of America." This composition suggests craggy mountains and a boulder-lined torrent. The plantings here consist chiefly of a windbreak of pine and spruce which makes a background for flowering cherries.

Next, one comes into the upper or main portion of the garden which is a water-dominated landscape with several typical Japanese garden elements: pebble beach, shoreline rock and boulder compositions, islands with connecting bridges, and a natural spring. The path leads to these major points of interest and conducts the visitor to the Meditation House located in an ideal spot for resting and enjoying the garden.

Plantings in this area include several shrubs native to Japan and used in Japanese gardens such as the Japanese

48

The Dawes Arboretum Japanese Garden photographed in winter.

PHOTO BY ALAN D. COOK

yew (*Taxus cuspidata*), kerria (*Kerria japonica*), flowering quince (*Chaenomeles speciosa*), Japanese maple (*Acer palmatum* varieties). The climate of The Dawes Arboretum is more severe than that of central and southern Japan where the most important gardens occur. Many substitutions of hardy American and European plants were made including rhododendrons (*Rhododendron catawbiense* and *R. carolinianum*), Scotch pine (*Pinus sylvestris*), dwarf Norway spruce (*Picea abies* varieties) flowering dogwood (*Cornus florida*), Canada hemlock (*Tsuga canadensis*).

In the Japanese garden one may miss the massed color from flower and shrub beds characteristic of American and European gardens. But its purpose is to create an atmosphere of calm serenity, encouraging one to stop for rest and for contemplation. It is a haven of peace, removed as far as possible from the confusion of the workaday world.

In judging the work of Mr. Nakamura one should bear in mind not only the fundamental ideal of this kind of garden, but also several peculiar circumstances not usually associated with garden building. First, the setting is among a grove of trees set out as forest test plots, and the lake is designed primarily as a flood control reservoir. Neither of these major elements relate to a Japanese garden, but both are incorporated successfully into the design. Second, the 400-some large boulders which form a conspicuous part of the decoration were gathered from all parts of Licking County, transported to the site and placed by crane. Third, the construction of the Meditation House and the bridges called for skilled craftsmanship in wood and foreign techniques, but here again Mr. Nakamura found local men could accomplish the purpose under his patient direction.

"Thus this garden was built through the experimental efforts of so many people, using mostly indigenous American materials," Mr. Nakamura writes. And he adds, "If the visitor, sitting quietly in the Meditation House feels a peculiar fantasy in the environment, then he will become another part of the experiment." ❦

49

PINE BREEZE VILLA
SHŌFŪ-SŌ

THE JAPANESE HOUSE AND GARDEN
FAIRMOUNT PARK, PHILADELPHIA, PA

MARY I. WATANABE

A t Pine Breeze Villa, a 16th to 17th century-style Japanese house and garden form a serene yet elegant entity, in a location which is both harmonious and historic. Aesthetically, the villa benefits from the slopes and expanses, the magnificent large old trees and other plantings of the surrounding areas of Fairmount Park. Historically, the site is important in the development of Japanese architecture and landscape design in America. This section of Fairmount Park has had Japanese landscaping and a Japanese structure almost continuously since the last quarter of the 19th century. During the 1876 Centennial Exposition in Philadelphia, the Japanese bazaar was across the street from the current site. The garden, associated with the bazaar, was probably the first Japanese garden in America. From 1905 until a fire in 1955, a 300-year old

MARY I. WATANABE, *President, Friends of the Japanese House and Garden, Philadelphia, PA is a retired biochemist. She has been a lecturer in Japanese at the University of Pennsylvania.*

Japanese temple gate originally exhibited at the 1904 Louisiana Purchase Exposition in St. Louis stood there. Shofu-so has been at the site since 1958.

The *shoin-zukuri* (deck-style construction) house, with an adjoining teahouse for the formal tea ceremony, was designed by the contemporary Japanese architect, Junzo Yoshimura. It was exhibited at the Museum of Modern Art, New York, in 1954-55, and subsequently given to the City of Philadelphia. The garden, appropriate to the house and terrain, was designed by Tansai Sano.

Under the direction of architect George Shimamoto, the house underwent extensive repairs in 1976, made possible by a Bicentennial gift from the government the Japanese government and people. Later, rejuvenation of the garden began, supervised by landscape architect Masao Kinoshita. Although repairs, replacements and additions of plants, and other changes have occurred, Sano's design for the traditional landscape garden remains: the intimate relationship between house and garden

is evident; the layout and landscaping create, in a limited space, the effects of depth and scale; the small hills, rocks, water and trees recall the mountains, streams, lakes and forests of Japan; and the garden integrates the house with its Fairmount Park setting.

The villa occupies about one acre, almost half of which is the pond of the main garden. A solid, white plaster wall with dark, Japanese tile coping, encloses the northern and western sides of the compound. The other boundaries behind the pond are open, permitting views which borrow from the outside scenery and landscaping of Fairmount Park.

The main entry to the villa is through a pair of wooden gates set in the northern section of the wall. There is also a special entrance on the south side for the teahouse and its garden. The grounds are landscaped on all sides of the house, but it is the southeastern view from the house that provides many of the elements of a 16th-17th century garden of a private residence in Japan: a large pond with an island; a stream coming from the rear of the house; mounds constructed to resemble hills; a waterfall; and carefully placed large rocks. The pond at Shofu-so contains *koi* (carp); the island, reached by a low wooden bridge, features a shaped pine (*Pinus sylvestris*); stone lanterns and stone water basins are placed at appropriate spots of the villa.

At Shofu-so, azaleas of many colors, rhododendrons, flowering cherries and other fruit trees, magnolias and tree peonies are the major blooming plants. Maples, pines, cryptomeria, chamaecyparis, bamboo, andromeda, yews, a weeping mulberry, a corkscrew willow, as well as holly, barberry, bayberry, euonymus, are other plants at the villa serve to provide a predominantly green garden. Except for grass in the back garden and on the mounds, the major groundcover is pachysandra.

The garden of Pine Breeze Villa is one to be enjoyed from the verandas and the rooms, but stepping stones permit strolling through various sections of the garden. 🍂

SANSHO-EN

THE GARDEN OF THREE ISLANDS

KRIS S. JARANTOSKI

Chicago Botanic Garden's Sansho-En, is a promenade style garden, which invites visitors to meander along winding paths and slowly discover the beauty of its 17 acres. The

KRIS S. JARANTOSKI, *Assistant Director of the Chicago Botanic Garden, worked closely with K. Kawana on the development of Sansho-En and currently oversees the maintenance of the garden..*

unique garden plan featuring three islands was designed by Dr. Koichi Kawana and was dedicated in 1982.

The large northernmost island, Horai-jima (Island of Everlasting Happiness), is a rolling, sparsely planted landscape inaccessible to visitors—to be viewed from a distance. On cold autumn mornings mist shrouds it. The middle island, Seifuto (Island of Clear, Pure Breeze),

Chicago's Sansho-En — Two of the islands are accessible by bridge. One is to be viewed from afar.

PHOTOS BY KRIS JARANTOSKI

The Shoin building is cantilevered over the water. Here it is shrouded in fog.

contains a rustic arbor. Nearby water trickles into a basin next to an *oribe* lantern. All this is hidden behind a small pine forest in the *miegakure* or "seen and hidden" style. A boat landing (*funatsuki-ishi*) is composed of two large slabs of granite. Keiunto (Island of the Auspicious Cloud) is the southernmost, largest and highest of the three islands. There, the umbrella arbor, offers visitors a chance to relax on porcelain stools of Chinese style. The adjacent dry garden contains bush clover, hydrangea and boxwood and is defined by a mixed hedge of holly, privet and flowering quince. The Shoin building, designed after the summer home of a Japanese feudal lord and nestled in an inlet on Keiunto, is the focal point of Sansho-en. The lush moss garden adjacent to it with water basin,

yukimi lantern, and hostas, is surrounded by an arborvitae hedge.

Sansho-En's subtle, refined elegance is softly punctuated by seasonal changes. Rolling hills of pink azaleas, cherry and plum trees, forsythia and crabapples announce the arrival of spring. Flowers of eulalia grass (*Miscanthus*) and bush clover (*Lespedeza*) along with ripening persimmons and the blazing foliage of maples, euonymus and viburnum foretell the coming of winter in the continuous rhythm of nature. Pines, yews and boxwood soften the Chicago winter and enhance the frequent snowfalls.

Sansho-En is a compilation of many styles of Japanese garden design which stirs the imagination, integrates people and nature, restores the heart and brings peace to the soul. 🍒

THE JOHN P. HUMES
JAPANESE
STROLL GARDEN
MILL NECK, NY

STEPHEN A. MORRELL

A hill garden

A tea garden

The John P. Humes Stroll Garden was created by a Japanese landscape designer and his wife in 1960-62. In 1983 the garden was donated to the adjoining North Shore Wildlife Sanctuary.

In keeping with the Japanese reverence for nature, the garden harmoniously blends the contrived and the natural. Using the existing topography to suggest the garden design, the sloping and forest land was transformed into an idealized landscape of mountains, streams and ocean. Gravel paths mimic mountain streams and form areas to pause. The path leads to the pond at the base of the hill. Vistas reveal themselves in sequence.

The design centers around a teahouse which offers a quiet retreat. Its garden provides a tranquil atmosphere using mostly evergreen plants, ferns and moss.

Plants in the outer stroll garden are a blending of existing native flora and indigenous Japanese plants, and reflect the changes in season so revered by the Japanese. With early spring come the delicate hues of cherry blossoms, followed by azaleas. Early summer brings a display of Japanese iris. During autumn, both native and Japanese maples turn brilliant reds, oranges and yellows. Winter snow highlights the outlines of trees and lantern tops and makes designs on fences.

SEIWA-EN

MISSOURI BOTANICAL GARDEN

ALAN P. GODLEWSKI

Drum bridge in Seiwa-en.

eiwa-en, meaning "garden of pure, clear harmony and peace," occupies over 14 acres making it one of the largest Japanese gardens in North America. The garden is the result of a masterful design by Professor Koichi Kawana. The basic style of the garden is "strolling" garden (*chisen-*

ALAN P. GODLEWSKI *was Chairman of the Department of Horticulture at Missouri Botanic Garden in St. Louis.*

kaiyushiki). Gardens of this style have a lake as their main feature and were popular among Japanese feudal lords of the 17th and 18th centuries. The other facet of their design is extensive lawn areas which relate an expansive feeling.

The 4 1/2 acre lake in Seiwa-en is irregular in its configuration, which permits vistas from divergent locations around the perimeter. A series of panoramas are revealed including four islands.

Tortoise Island and Crane Island are auspicious symbols of immortality and happiness, Paradise Island is a three-rock arrangement projecting from the water near Crane Island. This island celebrates happiness and immortality, and is the spiritual center of the garden.

The fourth island, called *Nakajima* or Middle Island, is accessible by two foot bridges. When *taikobashi* or drum bridge, is reflected in the lake's surface, it outlines a circle. The second bridge, a *dobashi*, or earthen bridge, is a low bridge constructed over a timber framework which is edged in mondo grass. The Middle Island also houses the teahouse, a structure which was built in Japan and given by Missouri's sister state Nagano Prefecture.

Several styles of stone lanterns are also used in the garden including the snow-viewing lanterns, or *yukimi-doro*. Two are preserved from the Japanese Imperial Exhibit at the 1904 World's Fair and another is a gift of Suwa City, Japan, the sister city to St. Louis. Another lantern projects out over the water with a slender arching stone base.

Seiwa-en is composed of plantings both native to Japan and Missouri. The framework of the garden is large oaks, cypress and black tupelo. Other plants are Japanese black pine, Kwanzan cherry, Japanese maple, star magnolia, and Japanese holly. These plantings are subtle arrangements of texture and color which are highlighted by seasonal display: spring is announced with weeping cherries, peonies and azaleas; summer with Japanese iris and lotus; fall by the brilliant colors of the oak, hickory, black tupelo and chrysanthemums; and winter is delineated by snow held upon the branches of the trained trees and the snow-viewing lanterns. This Japanese garden is a garden for all seasons. 🍃

Zig-zag bridge (yatsuhashi).

Armistead Browning and William Frederick traveled together and studied Japanese gardens in the Kyoto area for two weeks in 1981. Because of their similar exposure to Japanese gardens but their different landscape design philosophies, we posed this question to each as practicing landscape designers in America: "What can we learn from Japanese gardens?"

Both have several answers to that question. — The Editors

LESSONS FOR AMERICANS TO LEARN FROM JAPANESE GARDEN DESIGNERS

PART I

WILLIAM H. FREDERICK, JR.

The current trend toward lifting elements of an authentic Japanese garden and placing them in our alien setting offends my sense of appropriateness. To create and appreciate a Japanese garden one must have grown up in Japan, known the famous Japanese landscapes that have inspired these gardens, been part of a religious tradition that is highly disciplined, contemplative and ascetic, and been part of a society where much communication is

WILLIAM H. FREDERICK JR. *is a landscape architect who has specialized in American residential garden design for over 35 years. His firm, Private Gardens, Inc., is in Hockessin, DE. He is the author of* **100 Great Garden Plants**.

by symbol. Can you imagine the average American pausing to contemplate the view from each stepping stone in his garden? I can't. On the other hand, I'm always delighted when a client goes to Japan to study their gardens — there is much to be learned.

The Yen for Japanese Gardens

I've tried to figure out why Americans want Japanese gardens and have come up with two possible reasons:

1. There is the notion they are low maintenance both because inanimate materials such as rocks and sand are major elements and because plants are relatively unimportant to the composi-

58

tion. This is a misconception. Sand must be raked after every rain and kept free from leaves and litter, and plants are important. Moss, often a major element, requires time-consuming effort to get it to thrive. Shrubs must be trimmed to conform to previously established mounded shapes and sizes. Trees must be trained into a particular shape (one of several important styles) and kept in that form. Remember, those Japanese gardens one sees in photographs for the most part belong to either the Imperial Family which has the wherewithal to employ professional gardeners of the highest skills or religious orders whose members have an abundance of time and dedication.

2. There is a feeling of peacefulness and strength in the photographs of the better gardens. (Not all Japanese gardens are great works of art.) This has an understandable appeal to Americans leading pressured and harassed lives. To me, if this is what is wanted from the garden, one should analyze how to produce these sensations in a manner that is appropriate for our times in our locale.

I'm also not convinced that "peacefulness" is the total answer to the modern American's needs, at least not the majority. Strong design as a framework is essential and in the case of the majority, this should be fleshed out with exuberance rather than asceticism.

Important Lessons

The Japanese have probably spent more time than any other nationality thinking about and developing a gardening tradition. Some of the important things to be learned from them are:

1. THE ARCHITECTURE AND THE LANDSCAPE ARCHITECTURE ARE DESIGNED AS A UNIFIED WHOLE. Every important room of the palace, temple or house is intimately associated with the garden.

2. THE PERSONALITY OF THE SITE AND COMMUNITY HAS A STRONG INFLUENCE ON THE TOTAL DESIGN INCLUDING THE SITING OF THE ARCHITECTURE, THE DEVELOPMENT OF GARDEN EXPERIENCES, AND THE TRADITIONAL "BORROWING OF SCENERY." Much of our own site development involves insensitive destruction of trees, rocks, interesting contours on the premise that it is more economic to "clear and level" with "new planting" to follow.

3. AESTHETICS ARE A PRIME CONSIDERATION IN THE PLAN FOR THE ARCHITECTURE AND LANDSCAPE. This is accomplished by:
- blocking out distracting views
- creating the feeling of more space than there really is by manipulating scale
- limiting the number of materials involved
- making some open spaces (water, sand, lawn, pebbles, groundcover) have strong design forms
- reducing the complexity of the design to minimal abstractions (Reductivism)
- displaying a sensitivity to "occult balance"

Occult balance is another name for harmonious asymmetry (as opposed to bilateral symmetry). An understanding of occult balance in particular has important application in providing strength to the informal designs which often seem most appropriate to our contemporary life style. Such an understanding is not a mysterious gift of the talented few but simply a matter of training one's eye. Walter Beck (the creator of the American "Chinese Cup Garden" at Innisfree) engaged his guests in an after dinner diversion to sharpen their perception of occult balance. Three objects (such as three pebbles or a salt shaker, ashtray, and cigarette box) were placed on a cof-

Japanese gardens provide a series of experiences. This one is provided by water, gravel, rock and blooming iris.

fee table. Each guest, in turn, arranged them in a manner which brought them into a state of repose with each other (from his or her viewpoint). The remaining guests then expressed their feelings of gratification or dissatisfaction and were expected to explain why. We all do this more or less unconsciously as we react to composition in painting and sculpture, choreography in ballet, and the massing of forms in contemporary architecture.

4. FINALLY, THE JAPANESE "STROLL GARDEN" WITH A CLEARLY DEFINED CIRCULATORY PATH IL-LUSTRATES HOW TO LEAD ONE THROUGH A SERIES OF GARDEN EX-PERIENCES AND MAKE MAXIMUM USE OF THE SPACE AVAILABLE. In some of the best English gardens, such as Hidcote and Sissinghurst, one is "direct-ed" through a sequence of garden rooms providing separate and distinct experi-ences with sculpture, water and color

The blossoms of the weeping cherry are repeated in the reflective water of the pond.

and textural changes. Even in suburban America we are not without the experience of "walking around the yard" after supper. Because much of contemporary American garden design starts with a functional basis (car arrival area, entrance garden, outdoor living area, swimming pool garden, kitchen garden), we have the opportunity for a series of distinctly different, refreshing experiences and the Japanese tradition of the stroll garden has much to teach us about unifying these parts into a strong whole.

To see positive examples of these teachings in contemporary gardens:

● Look at the work of Ed Bye for indoor/outdoor relationships and reductivism applied to elements in the natural landscape producing moods of peacefulness and strength.[1, 2]

● Look at James Rose's house-garden relationships where the house becomes a series of garden pavilions and the merging of indoors and outdoors is nearly imperceptible.[1,3]

● Look at Thomas Church's gardens where the personality of the site and the owners is the design basis and reductivism and strong design forms are paramount.(4)

● Study the relationship of Spirit Path and the highly color-charged flower garden in Beatrix Farrand's garden created in Seal Harbor for the Rockefeller Family. This is a Stroll Garden successfully linking the extremes of spirituality and exuberance.[1]

● Study photographs of contemporary South American gardens by Roberto Burle Marx where design strength is achieved through a reductivism expressed in abstract color and textural forms related in sophisticated occult balance and where the "stroll" is through a three-dimensional piece of sculptured garden.[5,6,7]

●Visit the Abby Aldrich Rockefeller Sculpture Garden at the Museum of Modern Art in New York, designed by Philip Johnson. This Stroll Garden can hold large numbers of people and works of art. In its most recent form there is a strong indoor/outdoor relationship to the galleries themselves and, as in its original conception, there is a finely tuned occult balance in each of its several areas; a fine tuning of scale which gives the feeling of being in a residential setting; and strong and economical linkage of all the parts.[8]

Conclusion

I make the plea that we study the principles developed by Japanese garden designers over the years; that we apply these principles to developing a kind of garden design that not only responds to our own culture, but to our specific house sites and personalities. The tempo of our daily lives and the insecurities of our world situation call for strong medicine in our garden design and I feel this can best be accomplished by a variety of experiences, some of exuberance, within the same garden. This can only work on a framework of design strength about which we have much to learn from our friends in Japan. 🍃

[1] Built Landscapes, Gardens in the Northeast, (Catalog of a traveling exhibition produced by Brattleboro Museum and Art Center); 1984.

[2] Bye, A.E., Art Into Landscape, Landscape Into Art, PDA Publishers, Mesa, AZ, 1983.

[3] Rose, James C., Creative Gardens, Reinhold Publishing, New York, 1958.

[4] Church, Thomas, Grace Hall, and Michael Laurie, Gardens are for People, (Second Ed.), McGraw-Hill, New York, 1983.

[5] Bardi, P.M., The Tropical Gardens of Burle Marx, Reinhold Publishing, New York, 1964.

[6] Carter, Allen, "Gardens: The Hidden Valley," ARCHITECTURAL DIGEST, March, 1980, pp. 114-119.

[7] Gregory, Frederick L. "Roberto Burle Marx: The Brazilian Extravaganza," LANDSCAPE ARCHITECTURE, May 1981, pp. 346-357.

[8] Kassler, Elizabeth B., Modern Gardens and the Landscape, The Museum of Modern Art, New York, 1964, pp. 36, 48-49, 53, 62-63, 66-67.

[9] Ibid. pp. 58-59.

PART II

ARMISTEAD BROWNING, JR.

I t isn't an exaggeraton to say that Americans are obsessed with Japanese gardens. Hardly a month passes without another magnificent book on Japanese gardens appearing in the book stores. Articles on Japanese gardens are appearing with increasing frequency in magazines. The first Brooklyn Botanic Garden handbook on Japanese gardens went through six printings from 1961 to 1979.

And we build them. Sadly none of them really look right. It is both a harsh truth and perhaps the most profound lesson conveyed to us by Japanese gardens that the only place they work really well is in Japan. Wedded to their environment, they are both an expression of one of the most powerful cultural traditions the world has ever seen and a distillation of a spectacular landscape at once dramatic and delicate. The overwhelming differences between American and Japanese culture and landscape, as well as differences in the way gardens are made and maintained, make it almost inevitable that a Japanese garden in this country appears forced or out of place.

The few Japanese style gardens that do succeed are either didactic or exceptional, independent feats. The former do not pretend to be anything other than a display of Japanese art principles for edu-

cational or museum purposes. They express the intangibles of Japanese landscape design while using elements of the U.S. landscape—an almost impossible job. The latter are the rare products of an individual's art and building process so brilliant that the culture and landscape of Japan are evoked along with the actual garden—an even more impossible task.

But we can learn from Japanese gardens, and there is a delicious irony in all of this: Japanese gardens evolve from a culture and landscape alien to ours, but they teach us truths that apply to our own Western tradition of gardening. We *can* become better garden designers and garden makers by understanding principles and techniques used universally in the creation of Japanese gardens.

There is another point to make about the great appeal Japanese gardens have for us. Despite the cultural chasm between west and east, something in Japanese gardens bridges the gap. The strong spiritual and philosophic messages conveyed by Japanese gardens somehow fill a void existing within our own culture.

The Japanese Garden

Store the whole world
in a grain of millet.

Zen Haiku

ARMISTEAD BROWNING, JR. *is a landscape architect and teacher of landscape design. After traveling and studying Japanese gardens in 1981, he taught a month-long course at the University of Delaware and has given lectures.*

There is one misconception about Japanese landscapes to bury forever. Japanese gardens are not miniature landscapes. Miniature implies merely a smaller version of something, as a doll house is a smaller version of a real house.

The most significant idea that should be mastered is the Buddhist idea that the whole of the universe is contained even in its smallest part, as the haiku above suggests. This principle is a guiding beacon in Oriental philosophy and creative process. Consequently a Japanese garden, in effect, encompasses all of nature. It acts as a summation of nature—of its parts, of its binding energies—not a reduction of it.

The concept of worlds within worlds is directly applicable to garden making especially in reference to a new garden concept—the so-called ecological garden, born of the environmental movement in the United States. Among other things, the new ecologic garden emphasizes or brings into the garden elements of the natural world such as rock outcrops, wetlands, dead trees, animal and bird habitats, not simply for decoration but as expressions of natural process. Ecologic gardening is an affirmation, a celebration of the processes of nature and is based on an understanding of natural processes and of the relationships between the component parts of nature: water, soil, decay, animals, weeds, seasons, moon and rain. Events and items in the ecologic garden act then as a summation of the natural world and the forces that hold it together, in very much the same manner as they do in a Japanese garden. Accordingly, an American garden maker in the new ecologic garden tradition might base the garden around an existing swamp (water), an outcrop of schist (rock), or a thicket of sassafras (plants). In the design process, the designer adds or subtracts elements until the garden is complete as a distillation or summary of nature set within its originating landscape context. In this way, the ecologic garden parallels the manner in

PHOTO BY BETSY KISSAM

which Katsura or Ryoanji act as summaries of landscapes. The manner of their creation and appearance of the products are different, but the principle behind them is the same. Both Japanese gardens and ecologic gardens respect the natural world.

Mass and Space

At the most basic level, landscape design is the creation of space using framing and enclosing elements such as plants, landforms, fences, ground plane and sky. Space is framed from all sides and from

64

Even in winter, garbed in snow, the Japanese garden is tranquil and evokes a sense of peace.

top and bottom and is enlivened by focal points and accents within the spaces and by views reaching out over the landscape and visually connecting other spaces. Movement through the spaces is created by the designer with paths and quickened by accents or views along the route. Although all the elements of the landscape can be utilized in the development of space (rocks, water, soil, landform), plants are of particular significance for obvious reasons of beauty and interest.

It is easy enough to outline one designer's skeleton version of the land-scape design process as I have done here and even to build spaces in the landscape. What is much harder to do — and this is the measure of success in land-scaping design — is to infuse those spaces with the mysterious ingredients that provoke an emotional response.

The Japanese garden often represents exceptional achievement in the development of mass/space relationships, which act as a powerful carrier of mood and feeling. The *means* by which this is done serves as an instructive, forceful example to garden makers in this country. Consider the first view the visitor gets of Sento Gosho, an Imperial villa garden, initially built in the early 1600s. The relationship between the placid, calm ground plane of the pond and the tumbling, turbulent enclosing masses of vegetation presses in upon the viewer, yet is held at bay by that polished mirror or repose. The visitor feels the power and mood of the place, caused specifically by the way the enclosing and framing elements of plant mass are built up and articulated. The rhythms and heavy masses of the enclosing plants are relieved by the pine tree acting as an accent, leaning in the direction of a lovely grassy clearing, itself framed by dense vegetation and by the pond surface. And finally, there is an absolute economy of means utilized in this composition: a pond, clusters of rocks used as accents, a leaning pine tree, a grassy patch, and masses of green vegetation.

The Idea of Journey

It has often been pointed out that one of the major differences between Western gardens (particularly French) and Japanese gardens is that in the Western garden everything is visible — there are no secrets. Whereas in the Japanese garden, although the route is clear, a part of the garden always remains hidden. There are secrets and mysteries which lurk just behind the visible: the garden viewer is invited to embark upon a journey of discovery. The theme of the journey has to do with the Japanese philosophic imperative, that of setting up gardens as vehicles to guide humans into an understanding of their oneness with nature, and so to the ultimate goal of harmony, peace and fulfillment. The Western garden designer can appreciate the procedures used in setting up the journey in a Japanese garden purely from a design point of view and as an instructive model to stimulate his thinking in the

building of his own garden.

To the American garden designer, the specific techniques used by Japanese designers to create journey may not always work in this country. What is important is the use of Japanese gardens as conceptual models for developing the *idea* of journey in Western gardens, using Western procedures and techniques. Imagine how the short trip from garage to front door could refresh the tortured breadwinner if the traditional concrete sidewalk to the front door was a progression as a garden of discovery.

The Role of Plants

One flower opens, spring everywhere.

Zen Haiku

Many Western observers regard the pruning, shaping and supporting techniques used by Japanese gardeners as excessive, manipulative, and distorting. From the Japanese gardener's viewpoint, however, the shaping process comes from an understanding of the tree so that its essence is revealed. In effect, the gardener takes away from the plant that which is superfluous so its final form reveals its inner being.

There is much that the Western gardener can learn from this. Not Japanese pruning, shaping and support techniques, of course - that is the product of 2,000 years of evolution in a different cultural tradition. But doesn't a better garden often result when attributes of plants other than bloom, color and the purely ornamental qualities are explored? Attributes such as shape, bark, winter interest, age, relationship to animals and birds and variation in form.

The last great lesson out of the Japanese tradition with plants has to do with simplicity and economy of means. Often the plant palette of the great Japanese gardens could be described as a few visual highlights against green tapestries and layers. The prevailing color is green. Blooming plants are few and far between. Too many would be a violation of harmony and would shatter the mood of peace and repose so essential to meditation and spiritual refreshment. Besides, isn't the beauty and delicacy of a certain plant that much more beautiful when it isn't overwhelmed by a mob of competing blooms and colors. As the introductory haiku suggests, one flower is all that is needed to suggest spring.

A Final Note

The country is ruined: yet
mountains and rivers remain
It's spring in the walled town,
the grass growing wild.

Japanese Haiku

Presently the world is in the grip of an environmental crisis. And at its fundamental level, the environmental crisis is a crisis in perception in which the unity between all the world's parts, the oneness of man and nature, has not been understood or expressed by the dominant cultures. As long as cultures believe that earth and humans are separated from each other, that somehow humans are cast in the image of the sacred, but the earth is not, then it's easy to justify the plundering of earth to supply a culture based on material goods.

There hasn't been a landscape tradition that transcends the Japanese garden as an expression of the harmony of earth's parts, the oneness of all of life, the respect and reverence due to all of nature. We are drawn to the Japanese garden without really knowing why, but with profound yearning. The garden is mysterious, green, unadorned, peaceful. We feel at home in these gardens.

Any long term solution to the environmental crisis will require a long journey in awareness. Doesn't then the Japanese garden embody both the journey and the destination? Isn't this its greatest lesson to us all? ❧

"SAND FOR DRY GARDEN"

Many of the articles in this handbook refer to dry gardens or sand gardens. It has been mentioned that the term sand is used loosely—it is actually gravel or turkey grit.

Washed gravel made up of uniformly sized particles can be raked into patterns but does not look satisfactory. By combining several sizes of poultry grit the proper combination of texture, light and shadow can be achieved.

2 parts "grower" size
1 part "turkey" size
1 part "turkey" finisher
(*Turkey grit is available through livestock grain and feed stores.*)

This mixture will hold the patterns raked into it while presenting the most pleasing effect.

ADAPTED FROM AN ORIGINAL ARTICLE, *PLANTS & GARDENS*, VOL. 17 #4, 1961

There is at least a little Zen influence in every Japanese garden. This is the one at the University of British Columbia in Vancouver. PHOTO BY GEORGE TALOUMIS

ZEN IN JAPANESE GARDENS

KIM SORVIG

The stone garden at Ryoanji, Kyoto is a quintessential Zen garden. Such a garden (and there is at least a little Zen influence in every Japanese garden), is difficult and risky to try to "explain." It is a matter of sensing, of feeling — the "Aha!" of insight. When asked to explain, shallow symbolism is tempting but misses the essential point. Zen is about experience; personal, direct and unifying, and Zen gardens are expressions of that experience.

Zen is a sect of Buddhism which places total importance on meditation; indeed, the name *zen* itself comes from the Sanskrit word for meditation. This practice is not the passive contemplation of an external deity or truth. Rather, it is a dynamic, still "centering" of awareness, in which one has insight into and direct involvement in "truth," "deity," or "universal energy." This awareness is "beyond explaining," and even Zen's own scriptures laugh at themselves and at anyone who memorizes or tries to read symbolism into them. Zen teaching is full of riddles (*koans*) that demand involvement, and one is often told to become

one with the riddle; then the whole world unites behind a personal response to the *koan,* often immensely humorous, and seldom other worldly. Nirvana, the great liberation, is to be found in *samsara,* the real-yet-illusory world of the here-and-now.

What, you may ask, does this have to do with gardens?

A garden is one of the most direct expressions of human attitude toward the universe and the living environment. Most Western gardens, until recently, have been based on the attitude that this world is one of sin and imperfection, from which an escape to a "paradise" is desired, or upon which an abstract ideal order must be imposed. Western gardens, by and large, are either idyllic escapes or geometric "improvements," and are very often highly symbolic of some heavenly or romantic vision, or of hierarchic order and power, or both.

The Zen attitude is quite different, and so are its gardens. By meditation one realizes that one is united with the whole world, but is neither so oppressed by it to want only escape, nor so all-powerful as

69

to try to impose one's will on it. As expressions of this attitude, Zen gardens show the touch of human hands that accept, understand, and are harmoniously involved in the natural environment.

In such a garden, symbolism is superfluous—not unacceptable, but only a paraphrase not to be taken too seriously. The rugged "island" at Konji-in, in Kyoto, crowned with an ancient gnarled conifer, is not "symbolic of" long life—it is long life! The fact that it *also* resembles the shape of a tortoise, a long-lived animal, is a wonderful gloss, but only a footnote. Mistaking this graceful, humorous counterpoint for the fundamental melody is common, even among the Japanese. One Zen writing refers to this sort of nearsightedness as "slandering the sky by looking through a pipe."

In a Zen garden, rocks are rocks; the art of placing them is best learned by "listening to them" until one knows where *they* want to be. A human teacher or book can only help open one's ears so that one hears the garden more clearly. Plants are likewise plants. And human artifice is also just that, human activity seen in relief against the background of natural elements speaking for themselves. Humans, too, are natural elements; yet we are aware of the world, and awareness shapes us and the world both. Thus, where Zen hands alter nature, it is to clarify the natural event (as when trees are pruned or boulders juxtaposed to accentuate their unique forms); or to show human relationship to nature (as when a clearly cut, squared stone is introduced among naturally-shaped ones in a path). Both effects are very powerful, enough so that people brought up on the Western idea of humans-versus-nature often find the accentuated result "artificial," again completely missing the point.

In the Zen garden, every element is the whole, and is whole in itself. This is not because the rock represents a mountain, or because the garden symbolizes the world outside. Rather, it is because of a profound belief that the universe, the human mind, and the smallest, plainest flower or pebble are governed by the same forces, so that the microcosm is a macrocosm. This pervasive attitude in Japan, to which both Zen and Shinto contribute, is easily misinterpreted by Westerners a superstitious or symbolic. It is neither.

Not every Zen garden, much less all Japanese gardens, fully achieve this quality of "being what they are," but there is usually a trace at least. It may be in the illusions which remind us that perceiver and perceived are One—the tiny courtyard that feels like a forest glade, or the small window revealing a few bamboo stems which makes one believe that beyond the wall there is a vast jungle. It may be in the integration of interior with exterior, through borrowed landscape, or through the interweaving of house and garden spaces. It may be in the *absence* of things which suggest human meddling — the lack of gaudy double-flowered hybrids, the emphasis on the lasting forms of rocks and evergreens, the gentle poverty of means, the local materials, the keen observation and faithful suggestion of nature's handiwork. Being what they are, everything is The One. Those masterful gardens which fully express this are characterized by an immensely resonant depth, and inspire attentive, energetic quiet.

But beware of the lure of explanation. What I have written here is rubbish; "useful lies," some Buddhists call it. To truly understand the Zen garden, sit quietly in one, relaxed yet alert, until all explanations are forgotten and you and your environment become "not two, yet not one." Then you will know what I really should have said. 🍂

WORKING FOR SONE-SAN AT TENRYU-JI

Claire E. Sawyers

Early one morning soon after I had begun working there, it was raining too hard to sweep the gravel walkways. I followed Sone-san (Mr. Sone) down to the lake to observe the garden. Looking across the rain-dappled lake to the rocks and trees that had taken on deeper hues, he asked me in broken English if I knew about the rocks creating an island on the far side of the water. Sone explained: the middle rock is the peak of Mt. Horai — the island of the gods and goddesses in Chinese mythology — barely rising above the cloud layer of lake water. While those, he indicated waving towards four low stones in a line, are ships tied in a harbor protected from a vast ocean. Sone drew the conclusion for me: this is the nature of Japanese gardens, within a few meters, a lake is two contrasting things simultaneously — lofty clouds and a vast ocean.

Through a ripple of events I became an apprentice for a Japanese professional gardener, Saburo Sone, curator of Tenryu-ji's gardens and grounds.

Many mornings, once Sone and the other workers arrived, we each armed ourselves with a broom made of bamboo

CLAIRE E. SAWYERS *lived in Japan for six years and later returned to work with the Sone Zoen in Kyoto. Following the Longwood Graduate Program in Ornamental Horticulture, she became Administrative Assistant at Mt. Cuba Center, Greenville, DE. She is guest editor of this Handbook.*

twigs and swept the gravel towards the center of the walkways and collected the fallen leaves. Miura-san, the most advanced apprentice, also raked the white gravel garden every two or three days to freshen the pattern. Sweeping took until morning tea-time. When Sone indicated it was time to break, one of the others would run back to the work shed and prepare a tray with tea cups and teapot full of green tea. Sometimes we sipped for a half-an-hour, but just as often, attempting to finish other work, we didn't break until lunchtime when we returned to our *bento* or box lunch of rice, fish and vegetable pickles.

Cleaning the paths was a frequent and predictable task, yet it provided no clues about the work lined up next. Jobs ranged from relocating a stone lantern in the enclosed garden of a subtemple to wiring-up bamboo poles around a dog pen for the head-monk. During those early spring months, we constructed two stone walkways, one circling a newly renovated pavilion on the compound's central avenue, the other beautifying monks' gravesites behind the main garden. We added several camellia and pine trees to the grounds; we dug bamboo shoots encroaching on the other parts of the garden as soon as they appeared; we drained and scrubbed the spring-fed fountain inside the garden periodically and collected the coins visitors had

Saburo Sone-san wears the traditional working garb: a simple shirt covered by *happi* and baggy pants.

A majestic pine grows in front of the main temple at Tenryu-ji.

thrown in. On one occasion we drained the large H-shaped reflecting pool at the complex entrance to plant sausage-shaped lotus tubers in the mud. We built several of the fences during the spring with fresh green bamboo and once we sprayed the famous cherry trees .

The Sone-zoen

I think Sone took me on partly for nostalgic reasons and partly so he could show-off his command of English. He had attended two years of college in Oregon many years earlier.

Sone and his two brothers were in the landscaping business together. His brothers as well as his wife and children lived in Osaka, about an hour away from Kyoto. Sone was establishing the business in Kyoto while his brothers built residential gardens and landscape projects in Osaka. He kept an apartment in Kyoto and maintaining the traditional apprentice system, his workers lived-in, receiving room and board as part of their compensation. Once when I was invited with them to a holiday party, I went to their Kyoto apartment for dinner before the celebration. We cooked and ate in one small room, while nontraditional bunk beds filled the other room (perhaps an idea Sone picked up from his American college dormitory life).

The Garden

On the rainy day Sone took me down to Tenryu-ji's lake and enshrouded Mt. Horai, the legendary island of the immortals, he willingly passed the rainy morning away telling garden stories that the other apprentices probably knew well from studies. Sone searched for the English to make certain I understood. Continuing with the rocks, he pointed to the opposite shore of the lake to the gray, jagged, lichen-covered stones which looked like a gushing mountain stream. It is known as *Ryu-mon-no-taki* which

Elderly women swept and weeded at Tenryu-ji. Their costumes resemble those of their male counterparts except for headscarves rather than male headbands. Everyone had tea together during breaks. PHOTOS BY CLAIRE E. SAWYERS

translates as "Dragon Gate Waterfall," the name of a waterfall of the Yellow River in China. According to a Chinese myth, golden carp struggle upstream in the Yellow River and if they succeed in ascending the falls they turn into dragons. Just at the foot of the waterless waterfall at Tenryu-ji, a stone known as the "carp stone" peaks its head above the lake's surface. There is a joke in this. In ancient China a person who became a government official by passing a civil examination was said to be a carp conquering the falls and becoming a dragon. The stone carp has looked longingly on the cascade at Tenryu-ji for centuries.

Sone went on to explain *shakkei,* or borrowed scenery, a unique Japanese landscaping technique. The stones of *Ryu-mon-no-taki* so strongly suggest a mountain stream, he said, that a visitor looks to the surrounding mountains, imagining the water sources. And so the mountains become a part of the garden.

Three naturally flat rocks bridge the lake in front of the waterfall. Sone explained that those stones bridging the imagined white water represent three sects of Buddhism — the Jugaku, Buyo, and Dokyo sects — thus they comment on religion's role in making life's difficulties surmountable.

Besides the distant Mt. Horai there is another rocky island on the near side of Tenryu-ji's lake. The sign staked on the mound reads "tortoise island" and with some imagination and Sone's help I could see a head poking out of the water and four limbs. The inanimate tortoise brings life into the lake, but more profoundly it brings longevity, since in Japanese mythology the tortoise lives 10,000 years. Tenryu-ji's tortoise island is

73

uniquely connected to the lake's shore by an ornamental stone bridge. Was the designer suggesting Tenryu-ji is the bridge to longevity?

From the lake's edge we followed a delicately channeled stream to higher ground and came to the spring-fed fountain just behind the Zen meditation pavilion. We paused beneath two massive weeping cherry trees within hearing range of the gurgling water of the fountain. For the few early spring days the trees bloom, the garden overflows with visitors who come to gaze up through the green bamboo lattice which supports the sky of pink petals. I felt the fever of the pleased tourists who captured the blossoms in their prime. When I commented then about how disappointed the late-owners must have been, Sone disagreed. He said the Japanese understand the cherry blossom's intense beauty is due to its ephemeral nature.

Tenryu-ji's History

Inside Tenryu-ji's garden, especially in the early morning before tourists arrived and while the monk's chimes and gongs softly penetrated the shoji doors, it was easy for me to forget the modern Kyoto I had just traveled through and imagine the characters in Tenryu-ji's past.

Arashiyama, the area around Tenryu-ji, was popular as a resort as early as the 9th century, according to Loraine Kuck in *The World of the Japanese Garden.* Courtiers retired to the spot increasing its popularity and historians think that when emperor Gosago moved to Arashiyama permanently, the garden of Tenryu-ji emerged. Gosago's grandson, Godaigo (1287-1339) grew up there and following the pattern, became emperor.

Eventually courtiers abandoned the villa in Arashiyama. It declined and by then General Takauji was attempting to overthrow Emperor Godaigo and succeeded in pushing him out of Kyoto. The Emperor retreated to Nara where he suddenly died. Takauji feared revenge from the Emperor's ghost, but he eased the situation by following a suggestion from Muso Kokushi, monk of the nearby Moss Temple (Saiho-ji). Kokushi proposed the Emperor's spirit be enshrined at his old villa and childhood home in Arashiyama. The result was the Temple of the Heavenly Dragon or Tenryu-ji. Muso Kokushi became head monk of Tenryu-ji, and some give him credit for the garden design as it stands today. Historians also debate whether the name of the temple refers to Godaigo as the "Heavenly Dragon" or alludes to the myth behind the rock waterfall in the garden.

Farewell

I worked for Sone two months, never really feeling a part of the crew since I was foreign, female, and wasn't living-in like the others. That distance disappeared when it came time to leave. On my last day of work Sone presented me with a valuable memento of Tenryu-ji: a calligraphy piece brushed by the head monk. The characters read shizuka or "quiet" describing a zen-concept, but to me it also described the garden. After work, Miura and the others took me downtown and selected a souvenir of modern Japan for me—a wristwatch. On to a prestigious restaurant where we dined in a private room, consuming at least seven courses. Over dessert the other apprentices gave me books on Japanese gardens. They had filled the inside covers with characters which wished me luck.

The farewell party continued until early morning, and after all the songs they knew had been sung, they called a taxi for me. As I waved goodbye out the cab window, I caught a glimpse of my "souvenir-of-Japan". If I hadn't been leaving, it would have been nearly time to catch the bus for Tenryu-ji. 🍃

K O I :
T H E
C O L O R F U L
C A R P   O F
J A P A N

Joseph S. Zuritsky

Koi are the same species of fish (carp) that live in many of the streams and rivers of the Continental United States. They differ only by their colors. In China, the cultivation of carp for food and later for pleasure goes back over 2,000 years. Written instructions on the raising of carp date back to year 500 BC. Carp was cultivated because it grows fast, is extremely hardy and thrives in most of the climatic zones humans inhabit. After the introduction of carp from Asia Minor

into China and then into Japan, the species started to attract interest. As time passed, color mutations appeared in the spawnings and these separated and then selectively bred to improve color and subsequently patterns. Thus, from the homely carp slowly emerged today's magnificent *nishiki koi*, or brocaded carp.

Over the years, the carp came to symbolize strength, wisdom, and courage to the Japanese and many legends grew up about their virtues. Since parents hoped their sons would possess the same positive traits as the carp, each May 5th, on Boy's Day, parents would fly one carp-shaped flag outside their homes for each of their sons. This tradition still thrives

Joseph S. Zuritsky, *attorney and business executive, has been a koi hobbyist for about 15 years and now operates Quality Koi Co.*

and May 5th is a colorful event with thousands of carp 'swimming' in the wind on flag poles above Japanese homes.

Koi can grow to be over three feet in length, weigh over 30 pounds (although most seen in gardens are about half that size) and live more than 50 years. They eat almost anything of animal or vegetable origin small enough to be swallowed as they have no external teeth. The finest quality koi are bred in Japan where raising koi is a $100 million a year business but the hobby of raising and showing koi has attracted thousands of persons in scores of countries.

Koi are bred primarily for the color and patterns on their backs because their backs are most visible as they swim in ponds. Koi are classified into color, pattern, and scale types, and although each type allows some leeway for originality and faults, the color, pattern, and body shape are specifically enumerated much the same way dogs are judged in the United States.

Each patterned koi is like a work of art; each is different, but as with art very few are considered masterpieces. Those few koi which become champions at the large shows in Japan *are* considered masterpieces and have sold for more than $20,000 each. The reason for the high values is that even the best quality koi do not reproduce high quality young in large numbers. Out of 200,000 newly hatched young, less than 200 will be of salable quality and often none of show quality. After the laborious task of culling thousands to find the special few, the tiny koi must be nursed through their first years of life when they are vulnerable to disease, parasites and predators. Changes in color and pattern also take place during this time.

Keeping koi healthy requires duplicating as closely as possible their natural habitat which means the water must be clean and unpolluted. A natural spring-fed pond is ideal as the water is continously changing and need not be filtered or aerated. Since conditions hobbyists must contend with are rarely perfect, artificial means have been devised so koi can be grown almost anywhere: homes, public places, businesses, indoors or out. Ideal artificial conditions include proper filtration, aeration, water depth, amount of shade, and adequate water changes.

In a Japanese garden, one might wish to keep 25 to 35 large koi (18 to 28 inches) in a pond measuring almost 10 feet by 20 feet with a depth of four feet. However, the natural oxygen level of this pond would not be sufficient to sustain that number of fish. To permit koi to survive in these conditions, the oxygen level of the water can be raised by either adding a vigorous waterfall or a mechanical aerator. In addition, if the water merely recirculates, it quickly becomes poisoned by fish wastes and decomposing food if adequate filtration is not provided. This can be accomplished by creating a biological filter in which aerobic bacteria in the filter consume fish waste and excess food, removing dangerous chemicals and purifying the water. The filter box should be constructed to route pond water through four to six inches of 1/4 inch crushed granite. Within three to four weeks the aerobic bacteria multiply into sufficient quantities within the gravel bed to filter and purify the water and will continue to do so if water passes through the gravel at the rate of two to four gallons per minute for each square foot of filter surface. Pumps should have about 0.1 horse power for each 1,000 gallons, so a 1-horse power motor should serve a 10,000 gallon pond.

Fresh water should also be added to koi ponds. Each week about 10% of the pond water should be removed and replaced by tap water. One way this can be accomplished is to allow a dribble of tap water to flow into the pond continuously with the excess water flowing into the overflow drain, but first find out if your water company adds chloramine plus chlorine to purify its water. If so, a system must be devised to remove the chloramine from the water.

Although koi can survive limited periods of temperatures as low as 25 degrees or high as 100 degrees F, they are most comfortable in 65 degrees to 75 degrees water with 68 degrees being perfect. Quick changes in temperature stress the fish and leave them weakened and open to attack by bacteria and parasites. Ponds made in the ground are insulated by the ground and their temperature changes slowly. The key variable in moderating temperature changes is the depth of the water; the deeper the water, the slower the temperature will change. Most experts advocate a depth of four to five feet although it is possible to keep koi outside in slightly shallower ponds (not less than three feet).

Most ponds are constructed of reinforced concrete, but PVC or rubber liners are also usable as is any water-holding container which won't poison the water. Ideally, ponds should have rounded corners for good water circulation, smooth sides so as not to damage koi scales, and steeply-sloped bottoms (30 degrees to 35 degrees angle) with a bottom sump drain to eliminate solids and wastes from the pond without putting them through the filter. Steep sides also allow the movement of the fish and the water currents to move heavy solids into the bottom sump. The sump should be made so that the opening of a valve allows heavy wastes and dangerous ammonia, which also collects in the sump, to be drained into a sewer or french drain. Lastly, for clearer water without algae (green water) a skimmer should be incorporated into the pond, and the pond should be built mostly in the shade.

Koi are normally bottom feeders, but by feeding them floating foods they learn to feed at the surface where they can be appreciated. With patience, koi can be tamed and will even feed from their owner's hand. The addition of koi into a traditional Japanese pond provides the finishing touch of life and beauty to one of man's highest artistic achievements, the Japanese garden.

Koi dealers to contact for further information and/or Koi:

ASAHI FANCY KOI, INC.
1051 W. 190th St.
Gardena, CA 90247
(213) 532-2020

CALIFORNIA KOI FARMS, INC.
3360 Gird Rd.
Fallbrook, CA 92028
(619) 728-1483

KOI BREEDERS
P.O. Box 4
Newberry, CA 92365
(619) 257-3653

NISHIKI KOI
FUJIWARA SHOTEN LTD.
313 Santa Barbara St.
Santa Barbara, CA
(805) 963-4224

QUALITY KOI CO.
1355 Bobarn Dr.
Narberth, PA 19072
Joseph Zuritsky
(215) 563-3336 (day)
(215) 667-7340 (eve)

GARDENA KOI & GOLDFISH FARM
816 West Gardena Blvd.
Gardena, CA 90247
(213) 327-2872 🐛

NOTEWORTHY BOOKS ON JAPANESE GARDENS

ELISABETH WOODBURN

Both historic and contemporary views of a subject frequently show the bias of their times. To examine a subject via words and pictures of one period and then compare these images with a later time period is often an interesting comment on history itself. In the almost hundred years between Edward S. Morse's *Japanese Homes and Their Surroundings*, published in Boston in 1886 and the large, beautiful volume of Kanto Shigemori's *The Japanese Courtyard Garden*, published in New York in 1981, the gamut is run from the early describer of a mysterious faraway land for fellow occidentals, to a Japanese describing small gardens for possible emulators.

The number of books published between 1886 and 1984 show the continuing interest of the Western world in the way the Japanese use plants and nature to create gardens. The greatest — and the first — of all the books on various components of the five styles of Japanese gardens was by Josiah Conder. *Landscape Gardening in Japan*, published in 1893 in Tokyo, was followed in 1895 by *Supplement to Landscape Gardening in Japan*. These tall volumes have color illustrations (Japanese wood-block style), 40 heliographic plates, and pages of

ELISABETH WOODBURN *delights gardeners with old and new horticultural books at Booknoll Farm. She has traveled to Japan and articles about her have appeared in* **Horticulture** *and* **Garden Design**.

detailed drawings of fences, ornaments and paving so extensive that no one since has provided such a wealth of detailed information. A second edition was published in 1912. A paperback edition, reduced in size and without color plates was published in 1964. Most horticultural libraries will have this work but it is becoming difficult to find in book stores. It should be examined by everyone who wishes to see the style of Japanese gardens before Western 'interpretation'.

There are several other early noteworthy books on Japanese Gardens:

European and Japanese Gardens with the section on 'Japanese Gardening' ('Notes to the Lantern Slides') by K. Harada was published in Philadelphia in 1902. It was edited by Glenn Brown for the American Institute of Architects. The illustrations and brief factual text are informative and indicative of the precise nature of the symbolism.

The Flowers and Gardens of Japan described by Florence Du Cane and painted by Ella Du Cane was issued in London in 1908 as a volume in A. & C. Black's popular series of color plate books. The author states that although there are many books on Japan there was no book giving a short account of the flora of the country which is so often called 'The Land of Flowers'. She also says that most of her knowledge of the gardens is derived from Mr. Conder's work. She makes no mention of Sir Francis Piggott's *The Garden of Japan: A Year's Diary of Its Flowers*, also published in London, in 1892, with four color plates of flowers and a diary-type text which gives accounts of the Japanese appreciation of flowers and gardens throughout the year.

Another popular book of this period was Mrs. Basil Taylor's *Japanese Gardens* (London and New York, 1912) with 28 color impressionistic pictures by Walter Tyndale. Mrs. Taylor also acknowledged her debt to Mr. Conder. The continued demand for works on all aspects of Japan was reflected in the several reprintings of both the Du Cane and Taylor books. In this country the remarkable Japanese exhibit at the 1876 Philadelphia Centennial Exhibition sparked an interest in Japanese plants and gardens. These early titles continue to be pertinent as direct reports of what Westerners found most interesting.

At the same time these Western publications appeared, a number of Japanese published books on their gardens. They will not be included in this brief list as they are not common, however, many delightful volumes exist in Japanese. They are frequently small, specialized works on such subjects as stone basins, stone lanterns or paving.

Increasingly, the Japanese works have become available, either written in English or translated for us. Some Japanese works appear with names of plants in Latin or English, with perhaps a page of introduction in English as in the exquisite volume *Japanese Alpine Plants*, illustrations by Bunsai Ioki, with introduction and notes by Hideaki Ohba. This folio volume of 99 color plates of plants from Bunsai Ioki's rock garden was painted at the end of the 19th century and only recently published. It is interesting to note that because of the botanical accuracy of the plates, the Japanese feel this book shows Western influences.

Between the two World Wars there were several books published which were widely distributed. The following titles are mentioned for their lasting interest. Jiro Harada's *The Gardens of Japan*, which described the gardens chronologically, was well illustrated being one of The Studio Books and was published in London in 1928. Tsuyoshi Tamura's *Art of the Landscape Garden in Japan* covered history, principles and design with plans and over 190 photos. It was published first in Tokyo in 1935 and then in New York in 1936. The familiar little 'Tourist Library #5' *Japanese Gardens*, by Matsunosuke Tatsui, began as a paperback in the 1930s and was being issued as a hardbound volume still in the 1960s. Samuel Newsom's *Japanese Garden Construction* (Tokyo, 1939) was beautifully produced and is still as useful as when it came out. Loraine Kuck's *100 Kyoto Gardens* contained a map for visitors to these famous gardens when it was published in London in 1935. It also had eight color plates. The same author's *The Art of Japanese Gardens* (New York, 1940) was informative and popular for years.

Shortly after World War II the stream of books on Japanese gardens started with such titles as Mirei Shigemori's *The Gardens of Japan* (Kyoto, 1949) with many photos including 16 in color. These make an interesting comparison with today's color photography in Japan. As the years have passed, the interest in Japanese gardens, as evidenced in the publications mentioned below, has increased in scope. There is a rough division in those which appear now, as the practical how-to-copy works, aesthetic appreciation, and guide books. Almost all the titles have elements of each category. Using these frequently blurry divisions, the following is an attempt to group some of the interesting modern titles.

Guide books such as Marc Treib and Ron Herman *A Guide to the Gardens of Kyoto* (Tokyo, 1980) is almost a model for what a specific, informative small paperbound volume can be. It is filled with background information, plans and visiting hours, both to aid in viewing and to remember. Two guides of a completely different nature are outstanding modern publications. *Imperial Gardens of Japan* by Teiji Ito has 210 pages of photographs (138 of them in color) by photographer Takeji Iwamiya and essays by several important Japanese writers. This sumptuous volume was issued in folio size in Tokyo and New York in 1970 (also later printings). *Katsura, A Princely Retreat* by Akiro Naito (Tokyo and New York, 1977 and 1982) is also a large volume covering one garden in depth with 94 color photographs, plans, architectural drawings, and a colored, folding map.

A book dominating the practical and beautiful category is Kanto Shigemori's *The Japanese Courtyard Garden: Landscape for Small Spaces*, (Tokyo and New York, 1981). Seventy-five of Kyoto's gardens are shown in 93 color photos by Katsuhiko Mizuno. The 81 architectural plans included give the perspective needed to translate the photos into usable ideas. This, too, is a very large volume, beautifully produced. A much smaller book in this practical category is Teiji Itoh's *Space and Illusion in the Japanese Garden*. It was written to show two techniques of Japanese garden design — "borrowed scenery" and "the great within the small" — and how to create their special atmosphere. It was originally published in Kyoto in 1965 in Japanese, appeared in English in 1973 hard-bound, and then as a paperback in 1983. Other useful books for practical garden planning are: David Engel's *Japanese Gardens for Today* (Rutland and Tokyo, 1959 and later printings) with many photographs showing specific points made in the text; Tatsuo

and Kiyoko Ishimoto's *Japanese Gardens Today, How the Japanese Use Rocks, Water, Plants,* (New York, 1968) with over 200 photos with accompanying text; and Samuel Newsom's *A Thousand Years of Japanese Gardens* (Tokyo 1st edition 1952, 2nd ed. 1955) which makes its point page by page with a photo on the upper half and text below it interpreting the ideas. A final title in this category indicates the international scope of interest in these gardens. Tetsuro Yoshido's *Gardens of Japan* was translated from German in 1957. It, too, is well illustrated by photos, plans and drawings.

The aesthetic, or interpretive view is, of course, well taken in all the above titles. Three titles give special emphasis to this approach to Japanese gardens. Mitchell Bring's and Josse Wayembergh's *Japanese Gardens — Design and Meaning* (New York, 1981) is divided into sections which cover specific gardens, their particular style and how that is achieved. Masao Hayakawa's *The Garden Art of Japan* is a volume in The Heibonsha Survey of Japanese Art Book Series (New York and Tokyo, 1971, 1981 printing) which especially answers questions of historic background and meaning. Lastly, Loraine Kuck in *The World of the Japanese Garden: From Chinese Origins to Modern Landscape Art* (New York and Tokyo, 1968, 3rd printing 1982) presents good historic as well as modern views enhanced by 212 illustrations (44 of them in color). A brief bibliography included is helpful.

A complete collection of books about Japanese gardens in Western languages would fill a sizeable bookcase and keep a collector busy for many years. The titles mentioned above have been carefully chosen for their helpful information and illustrations and because they can often be found in horticultural libraries. They capture a glimpse of Japanese gardens for repeated savoring. 🌱